Slay the Student Loan Dragon

Tips and Tricks on How to Conquer the Student Loan Game

By

Matthew W. Burr

New York, 2020

Slay the Student Loan Dragon: Tips and Tricks on How to Conquer the Student Loan Game

Copyright © 2020 by Matthew H. Burr All rights reserved.

Independently Published

Cover Design by Kiersten Tarkett

All rights reserved. No part of this book may be reproduced or transmitted in any form or by any means, electronic or mechanical, including photocopying, recording, or by any information storage and retrieval system, without permission in writing from the author and publisher. The author and publisher bear no responsibility for any consequences resulting from the use of information provided in this book. All content in this book was created for informational and educational purposes only. It is not intended to be a substitute for professional medical advice, diagnosis, or treatment. Always seek the advice of your physician or other professional healthcare provider with any questions you may have regarding a medical condition. Never disregard medical advice or delay in seeking it because of something you have read in this book.

Dedication

This book is dedicated to the family, friends, professors, and mentors that have provided me with the wisdom, guidance, sacrifices, work ethic and knowledge to persevere when not only setting and achieving "unachievable" goals, but also through the hard lessons of failure. I could write an entire book thanking every person that has made a difference in my life. Without all of you none of this would be possible. All my success and accomplishments I owe to the greatest group of people in the world. You will always hold a special place in my heart. Thank you for everything.

Table of Contents

SECTION 1 SLAY THE STUDENT LOAN DRAGON 1

SECTION 2 ON A MISSION TO MINIMIZE/SLASH YOUR SPENDING 9

SECTION 3 MEET THE DEBT DRAGON 23

SECTION 4 ELEVATE YOUR EDUCATION, EYE YOUR EXPENSES 35

SECTION 5 PREPARING FOR BATTLE 41

SECTION 6 THE LAY OF THE LAND: UNDERSTAND STUDENT LOANS, SCHOLARSHIPS, GRANTS AND MORE 49

SECTION 7 PLAN OF ATTACK 63

SECTION 8 HOW TO PUT OUT THE FIRE: DIMINISH YOUR DEBT 69

SECTION 9 FORBEARANCE OR DEFERMENT: THAT IS THE QUESTION 93

SECTION 10 UNITING THE KINGDOMS: STUDENT LOAN CONSOLIDATION ... 103

SECTION 11 THE IMPOSSIBLE QUEST: CANCELLATION OR DISCHARGE 109

SECTION 12 BANISH BANKRUPTCY 115

SECTION 13 THE DEFAULT DRAGON 127

SECTION 14 WORK TO THE RESCUE? 131

SECTION 15 KNOW YOUR OPTIONS 135

SECTION 16 HOW TO DEFEAT THE DRAGON 139

SECTION 17 FINDING YOUR HAPPILY EVER AFTER 149

SECTION 18 A STRATEGY THAT SLAYS 153

AUTHOR BIOGRAPHY 159

SECTION 1

Slay the Student Loan Dragon

Once upon a time, there was an ambitious young man. After balancing diligently working while attending college, he earned his Bachelor of Arts degree in Business Administration and Management in 2007 from a small, private liberal arts institution in Upstate New York. When facing reality after graduation hit, he had opened that dreaded letter outlining his student loan debt. He closed his eyes, took a deep breath and saw 5 digits that would immediately impact his life - $15,000. This student loan debt was on top of additional credit card debt and car loan debt as well. The young man made the decision to get to work right away taking a full-time job and a part-time job to start to slay the debt dragon which was quickly becoming a formidable opponent.

Feeling confident in his next move, he decided to advance his education further to earn a Master's degree in Human Resources and Industrial Relations at an out-of-state university. As graduation loomed, the same pit in the stomach feeling began again but this time the debt dragon had grown to the size of $74,000. With this wakeup call and his eyes wide open, he started watching his debt interest very closely. Each week, the young man watched the amount increase on average $100 per week due to the interest accruing. He was absolutely stunned how quick that amount could build. From that point, he asked himself why is someone else getting rich off my money? This young man was me.

I set a goal to get out of debt as soon as possible. The same budgeting and repayment model has worked for the vehicle I purchased and will work for the next vehicle and mortgage. This journey with debt has not been an easy one as I struggled and had to make sacrifices while figuring out for myself how to budget and make payments on my student loans. I had to learn how to balance spending with debt repayment on a monthly basis.

Paying off student loan debt is not easy. In order to pay off my loan, I lived on $1,000 per month for twenty-three straight months. The $1,000 per month included rent, utilities, insurance, groceries, basic cable, credit card charges and cellphone. It almost broke me mentally to sacrifice at that level; and I frequently questioned why I set such a crazy goal.

I understand that this plan (or one like it) is not for everyone. Not everyone is able to live this lifestyle for months or years. We all come from different backgrounds and have different priorities in life. The main takeaway is twofold. One is to really sit down and look at your expenses. Where are the opportunities to cut expenses? The other is to understand the difference between a want and a need.

Do you really *need* that gym membership or do you just *want* it? For some people that feels more like a need. For those who are paying for a gym membership and not going, they need to rethink that monthly expense. A $35 a month gym membership equates to $420 off your student loan debt in a year. For others, if you're going to the gym regularly for $35 a month, that's a lot less than eating out or going to the movies a few times.

This is where you have to look at your lifestyle and your expenses. Prioritize what is important in your life. My priority was living debt-free, until I decided to work on another degree. When I graduate, again my priority will be living debt-free.

Being strategic in how you make use of your monthly paycheck makes you truly become a budgeting genius. I normally pay all my expenses at the first of the month and live off very little to nothing for the rest of the month. For loan payments, I make payments weekly to ensure that the interest does not accrue and the majority hits principal, even if it's only a few dollars. Ensure you are putting money away into savings, an emergency fund and 401k match to save for retirement.

The fact that debt has become a lifetime burden fuels my passion for helping to educate others about their student loans. I see student loan debt as a lifetime burden on people in this country and it should not be a lifetime burden. People have become numb and accept the fact that debt is just supposed to happen in life. We need to recapture financial freedom in this country and break free from debt. Setting a strategy to become debt free opens up doors that most do not know exist. I want to see everyone student loan debt free, the right way.

I wrote this book to prove that you can borrow significant money for education (as overpriced as it may be) and that it can be paid back relatively quickly - with the right saving strategy and understanding your wants versus needs. I have never assumed this would ever be a lifetime burden and I have proven it through 3 Master's degrees. Once you learn to sacrifice and live off of absolutely nothing, you will have everything you want in life. The discipline will set you up to successfully plan and save for your future.

One of the biggest takeaways is to remember to ask the right questions to truly understand the fine print. Most people have no clue what the details involve. It is important to know for yourself and to teach others about interest and repayments.

The Value of a Good Education

Let's look at the investment in higher education and it's payoff. Do I think college is overpriced? Absolutely. Is it worth the investment? Maybe. That is a decision to be made at the individual level. Each degree I have obtained up to this point has been worth my investment because the return on investment has led me to positions that made it worth it.

Education should be viewed as any other investment: risk versus reward. Earning a degree should not be an irrational, emotional decision. So, ask yourself this: *Will this lifestyle and experience be something I value in the future? Is it helping or hurting me?* Take time to truly understand how these choices will impact the rest of your life. It is your future, and you need to make the choice that is in your best interest.

Remember risk versus reward: Is borrowing the money (taking the risk), worth the reward, whatever the reward might be? Education is an investment and your degree, and all that went into earning it, can be a tremendous asset throughout your career. Every degree I have received (to this point) has paid off with increased salaries, additional opportunities, challenging positions, and valuable connections to a broader network of alumni. Taking advantage of your access to these networking and opportunities are what you personally make of them.

Your situation will be different than that of your roommate or friends. It's okay if people don't get it. My family never truly understood what I was doing or the sacrifices I was making until I achieved the goal. I chose not to share my plans with many people because I found it to be ridiculous that people doubt that paying off this level of debt was even remotely possible, let alone in under two years. But guess what? It is possible! With the right plan, anyone can pay off their student loan debt.

SECTION 2

On a Mission to Minimize/Slash Your Spending

Breaking News: There was a time when attending college was not only affordable, but it was cheap. People worked summer jobs, fun and relatively easy ones at that, and with their earnings were able to pay most of their bills for the upcoming academic year. Whether they were a lifeguard, a babysitter, or working in a retail store, students used to be able to leverage reliable summer work to pay for the fall semester.

My recent discussion about student loan debt with a Project Management Consultant during a networking event reinforced how much the cost of college has changed in the past few decades. He told me about when he was in college and how he worked summers at a steel mill in the Midwest. He earned just as much as the full-time workers at the time. The money he made working summers provided enough money for a car, a nice apartment, and his entire tuition bill. He even had spending money left to take his girlfriend out! I asked him what he thought about student loans, and he said,

"Well you could take out loans, but there really wasn't any reason to do so unless you wanted to build credit."

The time period he was referring to was the 1960s, but I know people who had similar experiences in the 1980s. I know people my age who were able to walk away from college debt-free by working part-time throughout their college career, making reasonable choices, and with some financial assistance and scholarships. They put in work, lived smart, and earned their degrees!

So why do we now need to borrow $50,000, $75,000, or $100,000 in student loans to finish a degree? Great question! Because with today's cost of living, that's how most of us have to do it. I am one of these people, but I'm committed to slaying the student loan dragon.

The Increasing Cost of Education

On average, my MBA courses cost me $300-$400 every 11 weeks at a highly respected private institution. One problem that students (or parents) face is the astronomical increase in college tuition and "fees". What exactly are we paying for? What is the value of a college degree? What are all of these "fees" going toward? Universities and colleges have different fee structures based on activities, room and board, medical insurance, recreation, entertainment, supplies, books, and the list goes on.

This is what is commonly referred to as "the fine print" that no one ever reads. In order to understand it, you need to take the time to read it. Below is an example of some of the higher education fees and other charges that most people are unaware of, yet this information is money most of us will eventually owe.

Activity/Co-Curricular Fee: $45.00

Books: $492.00

Books: $750.00

Board: $2,472.00

Board: $1,550.00

Student Health Fee: $354.00

Law Student Resource Fee: $640.00

Education Loan Fee Allowance: $286.00

Education Loan Fee Allowance: $538.00

Personal Expenses: $945.00

Personal Expenses: $1,512.00

Room: $7,416.00

Room: $4,637.00

Supplies: $96.00

Supplies: $61.00

Transportation: $680.00

Transportation: $240.00

Tuition: $22,550.00

Tuition: $16,656.00

(BigFuture, Quick Guide: College Costs)

When you read through the financial breakdown above, keep in mind that this doesn't even include all of the fees; it's only a portion of them. Fees can also be associated with living expenses, dining expenses, healthcare, and other items students and institutions must pay for. These fees cover salaries, taxes, and other institutional costs. The double charges noted are for two terms combined. Do I think that some of these hidden "fees" are completely unnecessary and useless? Absolutely. Why do I need to pay for books twice in a term, once through the system and then when I order my own books through the bookstore? What about transportation? I have a car; I pay for my own car and do not park on campus. It's the adage that if you want to play, you simply have to pay.

I could go on and on about this all day, and I will outline the steps and research involved in more detail in Section 4. In the meantime, I will not complain about paying back these fees as part of my loans either. Why? Because I chose to take out the loans, and I knew what the game was when I electronically signed the paperwork. Remember that education loans are risk versus reward, and student loans come with many risks. When we borrow money for our education, we expect a challenging and rigorous academic standard. What if you do not receive a quality education? Has this significant amount of accrued debt a) gone toward a quality education that you've maximized the benefits of and b) prepared you for facing the workforce with the edge that you need? Or is the degree earned actually programmed to be graded on a curve, allowing everyone to receive a 4.0 GPA?

Furthermore, does the school provide quality assistance in navigating you through gaining employment? If the program is graded on a curve and the quality is not great, remember that it is your money and your future. Is it worth putting in the work? That is a decision you must make. For example, having access to a career services office is a tremendous resource. They assist you in preparing for the working world. They will not apply for jobs for you and they will not interview for you, but they will assist you throughout the entirety of the process. It's simple; you get out what you put in.

I'm not here to tell you which school to attend or what degree to pursue, but note that these questions should be considered when evaluating programs and the risks associated with the student loan debt you'd taken on.

The rewards from a reputable college or university are just the opposite. Students know going into it that the education is quality. Classes are not graded on a curve. The career services office works with students to obtain internships, network with professionals, and secure job interviews. Again, students will get back what they put in.

All schools have different formulas when calculating costs associated with attendance, but overall the definition should be consistent throughout the United States. Rates will vary based on state income tax, grants, endowments, out-of-state tuition, private, public, size of the university, salaries of administration, pension, healthcare, general maintenance, and location. A school in New York City is more expensive than a school in Northern Michigan. Private colleges are more expensive than public universities. Location makes a difference in costs associated with attendance. For example, does the school have a dorm or student housing?

As we review the 1960s to present, the increase in tuition costs is significant. We have seen a decrease in government subsidizing in higher level education, causing an increase in tuition rates. Also, as real wages have remained static, our purchasing power has decreased. The days of working a summer job or finding part-time work during the school year to cover tuition and fees is almost non-existent.

Chart 2.1 demonstrates the astronomical increase in college tuition costs since the first quarter of 1978. Yes, you read that right: a 1,225% increase. This information was provided by the Bureau of Labor Statistics. Is it believable? Absolutely. Additionally, according to Scholarship.com, "Students who paid $5,964 for their tuition, room and board in 1986-1987 might think twice about attending the same college in 2006-2007: The average price of a four-year college has risen to $18,445." And that was over ten years ago!

Any individual I have spoken to that went to college in the 1960s, 1970s, or 1980s can attest to the rapid inflation in college tuition costs. Just think: as we complain about healthcare costs rising at 634% since 1978, college tuition and fees are nearly double that increase! How can they attest to it? Many who went to college between 1960 and 1990 are now paying for their kids' tuition and possibly their grandkids' tuition. How much will tuition be for your kids or grandkids? Can we expect the increases to continue? Time will tell; however, tuition and fee rates continue to rise.

As costs on almost everything in the United States have increased over the past 50 years, tuition and fees lead the way. My personal thought on this is that college is now considered big business. There is no cap on what colleges can charge related to tuition and fees. However, it has not stopped everyone from attending college, turning it into a big business.

Chart 2.1

Percentage increase in consumer prices since the first quarter of 1978

- Tuition & Fees: 1,225%
- Medical care: 634%
- Shelter: 370%
- CPI: 279%
- Food: 257%

Source: Bureau of Labor Statistics   **Bloomberg** Visual Data

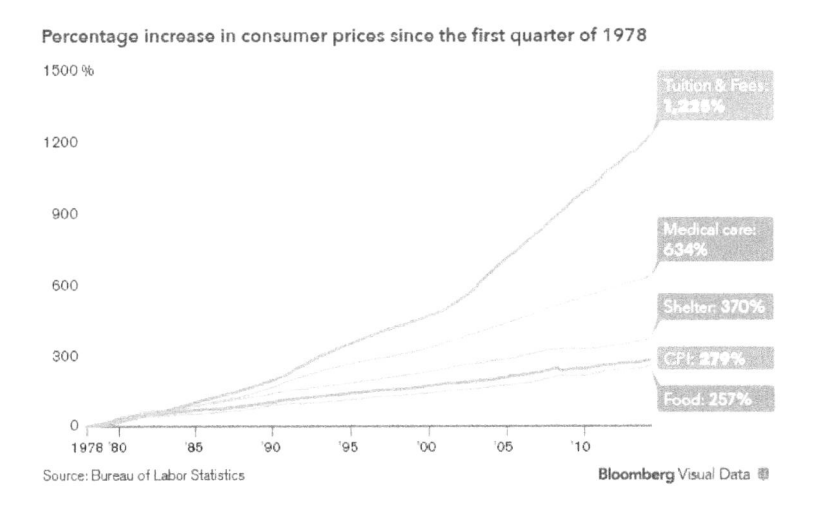

Chart 2.2, featured in the Bureau of Labor Statistics, is an example of the growth rate in college tuition related costs compared to other basic living costs in the United States. As

the prices of certain amenities for the house have fallen or remained stagnant, tuition and textbooks have seen the steepest increase.

Chart 2.2 Bureau of Labor Statistics

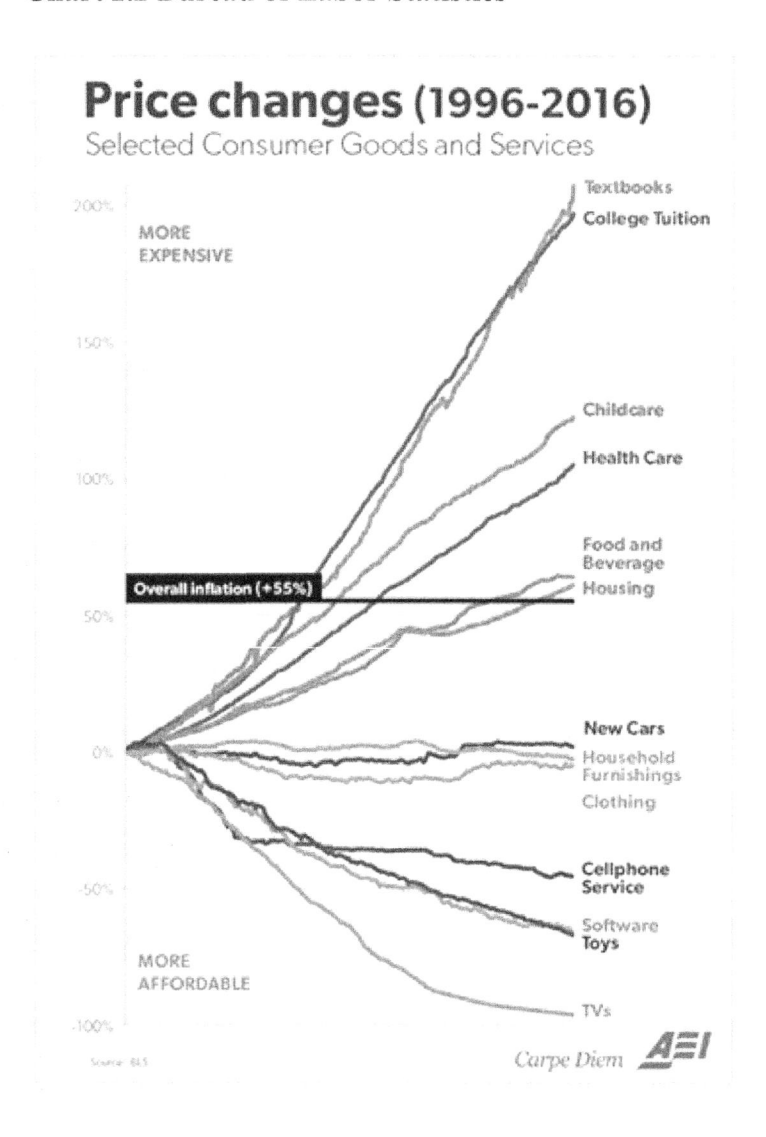

Price changes (1996-2016)
Selected Consumer Goods and Services

- Textbooks
- College Tuition
- Childcare
- Health Care
- Food and Beverage
- Housing
- Overall inflation (+55%)
- New Cars
- Household Furnishings
- Clothing
- Cellphone Service
- Software
- Toys
- TVs

Source: BLS — *Carpe Diem* AEI

Both charts illustrate a simple point: college tuition costs have risen at a more significant rate than any goods or services in the United States. Not even California real estate prices can keep pace with the rise in tuition prices. As investors in our education, we need to be aware of the tremendous price increases.

Chart 2.3 BLS Census Bureau

The chart below demonstrates how costs across the entire gamut of advanced education, medical care, homes, and the consumer price index (CPI) have risen since 1978 and will continue to rise.

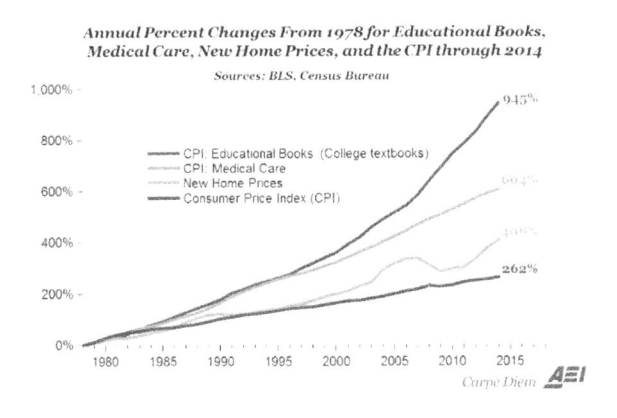

Annual Percent Changes From 1978 for Educational Books, Medical Care, New Home Prices, and the CPI through 2014

Sources: BLS, Census Bureau

(http://qz.com/792934/the-crazy-price-of-college-textbooks-is-pushing-more-us-universities-to-adopt-an-open-source-solution-including-seven-in-rhode-island-brown-and-rhode-island-college/)

The outrageous increase in costs are illustrated in Chart 2.3, regarding the costs of educational books, medical care, new homes, and the consumer price index through 2014. Textbooks have not risen at the same rate as college tuition, but at 945%, it is an imposing increase. And this is just up until 2014! Imagine what that looks like in 2020. I once had a professor tell me "there is no money in writing a textbook". I find that hard to believe. If that was the case then we would still be using books from the 1950s! Books are normally revised every three to four years, depending on the subject and material. With these frequent revisions, used books become obsolete and require students to purchase the latest and most up-to-date copy. Perhaps I should write textbooks instead of a book about student loan repayment? Either way, the information is always changing and second editions, like this one, can provide new and valuable information. The point is, do your homework on textbooks as well. Most professors and programs will post syllabi and book requirements on a website or homepage. Have a rough estimate of what books will cost prior to committing to a program, and investigate your options when it comes to textbooks.

Why do we care about all of these unbelievable figures? People need to understand the current situation we are in as a country as it relates to obtaining higher level education. As we grow and become leaders in our communities and throughout the world, we need to help others make choices as well. You are not only educating yourself but you could be educating a sibling, a parent, a grandparent, or a friend. The more you know, the easier it will become to make a proactive and responsible choice. Without knowledge, facts, and data, we are just making assumptions.

I made my choice. I chose to take on more student loan debt. If you want to play you have to pay, but playing and paying have a broad definition. If you have already made the choice and taken on debt, you too can recover and live a debt-free life. Here's how you can put out the student loan dragon's fire.

SECTION 3

Meet the Debt Dragon

The debt dragon is something that most of us are familiar with - the scary creature that is developed when we owe someone or some organization money. But just how scary is the debt dragon? We see the headlines in the news about how student loan debt is skyrocketing in the billions across the board with Direct loans, FFL loans, Perkins loans, Stafford subsidized loans, Unsubsidized, Grad Plus, and Consolidation. The amount of money that we as students and parents owe for advanced education is unfathomable. With each passing second, total student loan debt increases by $2,853.88 (FinAid.org). In the time it took you to read the last sentence, total student loan debt grew by $25,684.92. By the time you finish this book, just think what that number will look like.

The first edition of this book was drafted in July of 2016, but with every new school year since, new debt has accumulated. Fast forward to the Class of 2018, and the Student Loan Hero reports that 69% of college students took out student loans, graduating with an average debt of $29,800. These loans comprise of both private and federal debt. Meanwhile, 14% of their parents took out an average of $35,600 in federal Parent PLUS loans. What does this mean to you? You (and I) are part of these statistics. This information is not meant to scare anyone; it is merely stating facts.

Know the facts and understand how you compare to others in the same situation.

The student loan debt dragon can take on different forms depending on your own situation but most commonly comes in the form of direct loans to advance your education. In order to face the student loan dragon, some may enlist the help of parents, grandparents, or whoever else is helping to fund your education.

It's important to understand debt types to be able to continue to work towards a debt-free life. When becoming more familiar with direct loans, there are two types- direct subsidized loans and direct unsubsidized loans.

- **Direct subsidized loans** are available for undergraduate students with financial need. The school will determine how much you can borrow. The U.S. Department of Education pays the interest on a direct subsidized loan while you are in school and during the six month grace period or deferment period.

- **Direct unsubsidized loans** are available to both undergraduate and graduate students with no requirement to demonstrate financial need. The school will determine the need based on cost of attendance and other financial aid you receive. You are responsible for paying the interest on the unsubsidized loan during all periods.

The difference between the two types comes down to eligibility and interest payment during the periods. The financial aid forms on the FAFSA (Free Application for Federal Student Aid) website will provide you with the different options for applying for loans, depending on what the school will accept and what you qualify for at the time. I have gone through the Stafford subsidized, unsubsidized, and grad PLUS loans. It's important to remember that your credit score does matter—without good credit loan applications can, and do, get rejected.

Get to know your financial aid advisor

The private school I attended to complete my bachelor's degree sat down with my mother and I, and explained the student loans line by line, along with the costs. Regardless of the size or type of institution, there is no reason you can't request this assistance. Be proactive with your approach and backup the request with facts, data, and questions. As I have had a mixed experience with financial aid offices, I have learned to be very proactive in my research and in how I approach questions regarding my loans.

Ask question, after question, after question

When you meet with a financial aid advisor or a representative from the school, be sure to have a list of questions prepared. My experiences with financial aid and hidden fees have not always gone smoothly. Only one out of four schools I've worked with was upfront about student loans and associated costs. If you do not ask for the information, you will never know what the answer is or could be. As I tell my students in a class regarding job applications: what is the worst an employer can do if you apply for a job? Send you a rejection letter! If you never apply, you will never know if you could land the job or not. What's the worst a financial aid office can do if you ask for information? You guessed it! They can tell you no.

Electronic systems have made the application submission process more efficient and streamlined. However, the electronic system cannot verbally answer questions. So, when we borrow $60,000 to $100,000 for a degree, we need to fully understand where the money is going, interest rates, loan options, and loan repayment plans. Be prepared. The more questions you have upfront for financial aid representatives, the better your decision-making power will be in the end.

Leave no stone uncovered. After you've gone through the process once or twice, you should have a better grasp on the information.

Find a workaround

If a school is being selective or secretive with providing information, find a workaround. I define a workaround as finding information or getting things done through alternative channels. A workaround option for you could be a high school guidance counselor, older sibling, other relatives, friends of your parents, your friend's parents, co-workers, a sports coach, a current student at the school, an alumnus, or online research. Better yet, ask yourself if this really the place you want to go to school. Are they being honest or are they looking for another stream of income?

Keep your emotions under control

If the financial aid officer is being dishonest or withholding information, ask for a supervisor or manager. Bring facts, dates, times, and emails if you meet with a supervisor and keep your emotions under control. If you feel like the individuals you are interacting with or the school at large aren't telling you the whole truth, then it might be time to consider an alternative option. But before we point a finger at the person, have we asked all the right questions and received the wrong answers? Financial aid officers and loan advisors are extremely busy, especially at bigger schools. They might overlook certain questions or forget costs. We all make mistakes, which is why you need to fully understand information and be prepared with questions prior to the meeting or phone conversation.

Trust your instincts

If it's a scam it's a scam. Go with your gut. If you get a bad feeling, walk away. Do not sign any paperwork that day. If you need to think about it, take the time to think about it. Do not be bullied or forced into signing loan documents. Colleges and universities know this is a life changing decision for you or your child. Thank them for the information and set a date to follow-up with them.

Hold yourself accountable to committing to the follow-up date or communicating a decision. Ask follow-up questions if you have them. Do not leave any information on their side of the table. If the decision is right, you will know it. We all do. If you make a mistake, learn from it and move on.

Do not be afraid to ask questions and demand information that pertains to your future. Make sure it's the right decision for you or your child. Do not make any decisions based on irrational emotions, guilt, or uncertainty. Make a choice based on logic, with information backing up the decision. Know everything you can about the school, loans and process prior to making a choice.

Be your own money manager

I check my accounts almost daily to ensure I'm watching as money goes in and out and as interest is accruing. Who else cares about my future more than me? The schools will not manage your account for you and the government will not manage it, so make it a priority to check the accounts and check them often. Develop a routine or process to ensure you check the accounts.

The student loans are added revenue stream for the school, so once that revenue stream is over through graduation, transferring or dropping out, the school is out of the process. Care enough to understand it; it is your money and future earnings going into someone else's pocket.

Institutions must pay for maintaining the campus, marketing to future students, salaries, administrative costs, athletics, information technology, legal fees, and other expenses. Colleges also expect donations and endowments from alumni. These can go to a general fund or be used for certain activities. Again, know your institution and the specifics surrounding the school.

Federal loan revenue (when you are paying the money back) is used to fund branches of the government and programs. As I was researching, the interest money is used for salaries and benefits to employ individuals who then call delinquent nonpayers about their student loans. Basically, the interest that is paid is used to hire and employ people to find and harass people who are not paying the interest. I am not sure how effective that approach is, but reading the last few lines, it doesn't sound very effective or successful. You be the judge.

Evaluate your taxes

As I worked through draft after draft of this book I realized that an extremely important section was missing from the text. What about tax relief for student loan interest? This is something I forgot about, as I had never qualified to claim it on my taxes.

The IRS in most situations does not allow personal interest to be deductible on your tax return. However, if your modified adjusted gross income is less than $80,000 ($160,000 if filing a joint return) there is a special deduction allowed for paying interest on a student loan used for higher education. The deduction can reduce your income subject to tax by up to $2,500.

Qualifications include:

- The student loan must have been taken out solely to pay qualified education expenses and cannot be from a related person or made under a qualified employer plan.
- The deduction of interest paid during the remainder of your student loan. If you pay the loan for five years and earn under the modified adjusted gross income amount, the amount can be deducted up to $2,500.

Keep in mind that the modified adjusted gross income amount will change. In 2012, the amount was $72,000. What will you do with tax return money? That's right, pay down debt!

SECTION 4

Elevate Your Education, Eye Your Expenses

Chart 3.2 breaks down the 2016 level of graduate school debt by percentage outstanding. Going back to 2012, about 40% of all student loan debt was used to finance graduate and professional degrees according to data from a 2012 Newamerica.org study.

The 2012 study breaks down the combined undergraduate and graduate debt by degree:

- MBA: $42,000 (11% of graduate degrees)
- Master of Education: $50,879 (16%)
- Master of Science: $50,400 (18%)
- Master of Arts: $58,539 (8%)
- Law: $140,616 (4%)
- Medicine and Health Sciences: $161,772 (5%)
- Other Master's Degrees: $55,489 (15%)

The numbers are glaring. As these student loan debt statistics show, the cost of attending college is becoming a growing burden for a huge portion of Americans.

The focus as of late has been directed at the amount of debt one must incur to obtain a law degree. On average, a person borrows over $100,000 for a law degree. Masters of Science covers many degrees ranging from education to management. A law or MBA degree is specific to a field. These figures are a snapshot of the 2016 debt nationwide and the data will fluctuate as more individuals enroll in graduate schools.

Chart 3.2

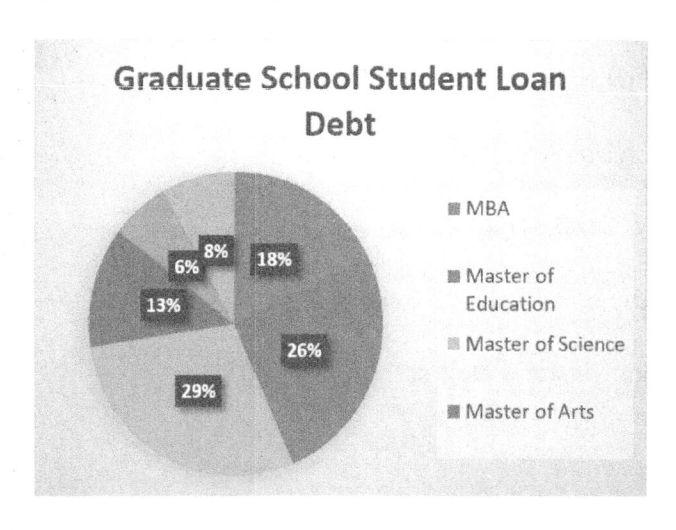

Graduate School Student Loan Debt

- MBA: 18%
- Master of Education: 26%
- Master of Science: 29%
- Master of Arts: 13%
- 6%
- 8%

(https://studentloanhero.com/student-loan-debt-statistics-2016/#)

Chart 3.3 demonstrates the average debt per borrower in all classes since 1993. This is a chart that should be of great concern to all of us. The amount of debt per class continues to grow and grow and grow. Earning a salary above $40,000, depending on where you live in the country, upon graduation is a great start right out of school. However, the amount of student loan debt is almost at that same level. My concern with this figure is even with a solid starting salary, a borrower is still drowning in debt. I know students that are borrowing almost $100,000 to obtain a bachelor's degree. Before they blink, they owe $100,000 for the degree. Can they recover? Can you recover? Of course, but it's always easier to play the game if you know the rules and the type of debt you're committing too. It is a complex and confusing process, and I am here to help you navigate the unknown of the land of debt.

Chart 3.3

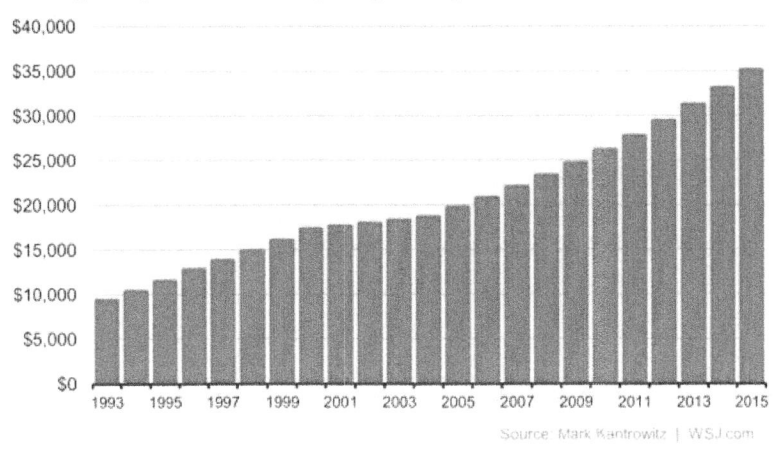

Head of the Class
Average debt per borrower in each year's graduating class

Source: Mark Kantrowitz | WSJ.com

(http://blogs.wsj.com/economics/2015/05/08/congratulations-class-of-2015-youre-the-most-indebted-ever-for-now/)

Many people pursuing a graduate degree are older, which means they are taking out student loan debt in their 30s, 40s, and even 50s. This is especially true when seeking a career change or advancement in their current field. However, consider the chart below, which shows the amount of student loan debt for individuals 60 years of age and older, from 2005-2015. As you can see, the number has increased significantly over that 10-year period. This is a concerning trend, as retirees are now living on set budgets and student loan debt is now an even greater burden on this population. Keep this in mind as you think about your future. Do you really want to be paying down student loan debt at age 60 or older? No! It's all about taking control of your situation.

Chart 3.4

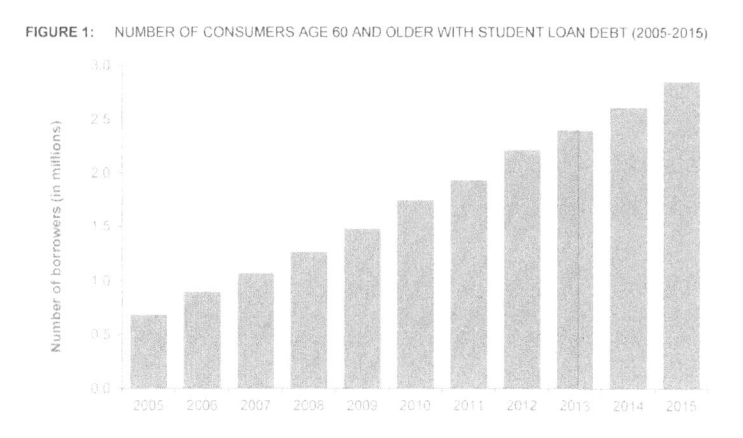

FIGURE 1: NUMBER OF CONSUMERS AGE 60 AND OLDER WITH STUDENT LOAN DEBT (2005-2015)

Source: Federal Reserve Bank of New York Consumer Credit Panel / Equifax

At the end of the day, when it comes to borrowing money to cover the cost of college tuition and all other related expenses, consider the loans you are taking out—whether subsidized or unsubsidized—before you make any decisions. Do your research because one thing that has also changed over the years is accessibility to information that will help you make an informed decision on the school and program you choose that best matches your career path and your financial goals. All of these considerations—the program, your career path, and the debt you incur—are intertwined and should be handled as such. Make sure that when you're looking to elevate your education, you are keeping a close eye on all associated expenses.

SECTION 5

Preparing for Battle

The costs associated with higher education can be hidden in the fine print. Every school has different charges, so the more you know, the better your decision making will be. Before you commit, do your homework! (I do mean that literally.) If you or your parents have been saving for college since you were born: well done! You have taken the first step in ensuring a debt-free college experience. Or have you?

The cost of a college education and the debt that goes with it are two problems that will not be fixed overnight. The more informed you are about student loan debt, the more resources you have and the better able you are to take proactive steps in ensuring financial freedom.

Research and visit each school

Review the website and reviews in journals and magazines. Connect with alumni and ask them about their experience. Talk to employees who work at the school. Check out resources such as US News & World Report, NACAC, and Forbes. Visit every school you are interested in! Pictures on a website can be enticing, or not, but being there in person gives you a real feel for the school. Culture is important and you will not know if it is a fit until you visit. This gives you the opportunity to talk to students, faculty, coaches, and different areas of support.

ROI & Career Development Centers

Career Development Centers or Career Services Offices are the best way to see the return on your investment when considering advancing your education. They will provide high level information on the office, staff, and opportunities. I recommend sitting down with a member of their team and asking questions regarding internship opportunities, networking events, placement rates, starting salary, resume workshops, interview workshops, LinkedIn workshops, and other valuable experiences. They want students to come in and engage with them because they are a tremendous resource.

Understanding the tuition costs

- **Living expenses** - Remember that on campus and off campus living expenses will vary. Research local apartments and housing options, keeping in mind that the traditional freshman is often required to live on campus.

- **Book expenses** - As book prices continue to rise, the school will provide rough estimates of book costs. My personal experience is that the rough estimate is extremely low and that in reality, books tend to be much more expensive. Research the specific courses and review the syllabus to understand what is required. This will provide you with more information to price books online on your own. Consider money-saving ideas like e-books or renting your text books for a fraction of their full price. Since you often only need them for a single semester, having a copy to carry around for the rest of your life isn't necessary.

- **Parking expenses** - If you do park off campus additional research will be required for the location.
- **Supplies** - Supplies will vary by course in your chosen field of study or general degree requirements. For example, for science courses where there are labs involved there will be additional expenses. Some classes will require different tools like graphing calculators for math, science, and statistics classes.
- **Travel** - This includes travel for sports, trips both inside and outside of the country, and job interviews. There can be additional costs that you're responsible for and you may not even realize it until you get a bill for $3,000. Yes, this happened to me with a Ireland trip, except it was $5,000.
- **Technology** - Be sure to take advantage of student discounts that school and many retailers provide.
- **Average percentage increase in tuition** - You might have to dig for this if it is a private school. Complete thorough research on the school website and understand what the average tuition hike could be

over the next four years. Recently I have seen many schools "freeze" tuition. However, they have worked around this with increased fee charges. Understand what all the fees and charges are that are associated with the program.

- **Average scholarships awarded -** This information should be contained on the financial aid and tuition website.

- **Scholarship applications** - There are thousands of scholarships to apply for. I recommend starting with the financial aid office and then pursuing additional options through your own research. If you are interested in a specific career, review the websites and see if there are options.

- **Healthcare costs -** If you are covered under a parent's plan, this is a fee that could be eliminated but remember to ask questions upfront. Keep in mind that many schools require up-to-date immunization records prior to starting.

- **Dorm vandalism charges** - This could be a hidden fee and one to ask about if you meet with the school. At times, colleges will charge everyone in a dorm for repair costs if they cannot determine who did the damage. I have been charged for damage other students were responsible for despite my lack of involvement. My parents were less than pleased with that charge.

- **Food costs** - Certain schools will provide multiple levels within the meal plan. Don't pay for food you won't eat, if you can help it. If living on your own, try to budget weekly/monthly to anticipate your expenses. Even if you have a meal plan, there still might be those items that you need (or think you need) to purchase on a regular basis.

- **Sporting attendance costs** - After all, we all love football and basketball games. This is a question to ask upfront if you cannot find information on the website. I paid extra for season football tickets. Certain schools allow students access to sporting events for free, some of which are based on a lottery system if the team draws large crowds.

- **Student activities fee** - I recommend having a clear understanding of what the activity fee covers. Ask for a breakdown and understand what is and what is not covered.

- **Fitness center** - Colleges have tremendous facilities available to students. Find out if there is an additional charge to use the fitness center. Many times, this is combined with the activity fee.

- **Student loan/financial aid application processing** - Yes, colleges do charge to process student loan applications, and the fee isn't small. I consider this a hidden fee and recommend asking a financial aid advisor what the cost is.

- **Clubs and recreation** - Volunteerism and community involvement are great opportunities for every student, and I highly recommend that all of us become involved in the community. However, certain clubs will have membership fees or travel requirements. If you are interested in a campus club or a recreational event, do your research and ask questions. Networking with current students, club advisors, or alumni will provide additional information.

- **Printing fees** - At times this fee is combined within the activity fee charge, but printing in a school library or computer lab can be an additional cost.

Clearly, there are a lot of considerations when it comes to expenses. I've provided you with a lot to consider, questions to ask, and resources to tap into so that you can best educate yourself prior to making a decision on a school and program.

SECTION 6

The Lay of the Land: Understand Student Loans, Scholarships, Grants and More

On the last student loan I signed for in July of 2016, the fine print was microscopic and four pages in length. It took me 20 minutes to read the entire document. However, I had a general understanding of what information was included in the document prior to reading, due to my love of borrowing money to continue my education. You have to know the lay of the land before making any financial decisions.

The fine print can be both confusing and extremely boring. In my own words, I will provide definitions to help you better understand it all. Is every loan document the same? Does your car and mortgage loan have the exact same contract language? What about your cellphone contract and credit card? Of course not! So, here are some details to sort through:

Federal Loans: These loans are backed by the federal government. They are often used by students for loan forgiveness programs and can be deferred until graduation.

- Federal loans include Subsidized and Unsubsidized loans, as previously covered in Section 3.
- When do you need to start paying? Six months after graduation. Trust me, six months isn't that long when you have $64,000 hanging over your head at the time of graduation.

Private Loans: These loans are issued by private banks. In most cases, these loans will not qualify for loan forgiveness and in some cases, you might not be able to defer the loans until graduation.

- What does that mean? You do have to pay back the money you borrowed—plus interest—and if you cannot defer, you might have to work during college and make payments. Work during college? Yes, it's possible, but who wants to do that?

Can you make payments on federal or private loans while you are in school? Absolutely, and if you can do it, I would highly recommend it. Debt is stressful, so the less money you owe, the less stress you will have. There are several types of repayment options available. Find one that works for your situation.

Fixed Rate: The interest rate is locked in for the life of the student loan, regardless of interest rate fluctuation or federal reserve policy. The benefit? Consistency in interest rate. The downfall? Taking out a loan during a time in the economy when loans are at a potentially high interest rate. My loans have always been fixed rate. The payment would not have changed over the life of the loan, but I would owe more money if I just made minimum payments. The only time a fixed rate loan will change is through consolidation. We will work through consolidation later on.

Variable Rate: The interest rate will fluctuate and change, depending on the lender. These changes can occur monthly or quarterly. Variable rate loans have both positive and negative attributes. If you prefer consistency in a monthly payment amount, I would not recommend variable rates. If fluctuations and changes do not scare you, why not look into variable rate loans? You might get a better interest rate, which will save you money in the long term.

Short-Term Payment: This by far is my favorite option. Pay off the loan as fast as you possibly can. That's it! Throw any and all extra money at the debt and watch it shrink. In this day and age, it's as easy as a swipe on your phone to send extra money to your loan.

Long-Term Payment: The government and banks will provide us the borrowers 15, 20, or a 30 year payment schedule. Really? Yes. These institutions make money off interest. They want you to take every bit of that 30 years to pay off your loan while they collect the interest. However, unlike a mortgage, there is no penalty for paying off your student loans early. Do you have the option to make minimum payments for a longer period of time? Yes. Life happens and sometimes we need that extra time to pay off debt. Evaluate your situation.

My recommendation is to pay your loans off as quickly as you can. Just because the paperwork states that we have decades to pay off the loan in its entirety, it doesn't mean that you must spend all those years in student loan debt.

Pause here if you currently owe money for student loans. Calculate out the interest versus amount owed over the 15, 20, or 30 year period. Or, find a website to plug in the total amount, interest rates and payment schedule. Below are two online resources that can calculate the interest on the loan.

- The SmartStudent Guide to Financial Aid
- Federal Student Aid Loan Simulator

The numbers do not lie, and these numbers should be a concern to all of us. Remember, someone else is getting rich off of your debt. Pay as much extra money each month as you can afford toward these loans. No, you do not have to make double and triple payments if you can't! But, adding an extra $20 more than the minimum per month, you will feel great about your progress and you will begin to make responsible steps to becoming debt-free. No, it isn't easy, but it is worth it. Now, go back and calculate the interest you will save over the life of the loan by adding additional money towards the principal each month rather than paying just the minimum payment. You should feel great about this. The momentum builds over time!

Since starting this journey, I have never made a minimum monthly payment on any debt I have had. I am not saying this in arrogance, I am simply showing my commitment to paying off my student loan debt as early as possible. It is a discipline I stick to. Other people are making money off of my debt, and I don't like that.

Here are some things to consider about interest on loans:

- **Subsidized Loans:** These loans do not start accruing interest before you leave school.
- Unsubsidized Loans: You guessed it. These loans do start accruing interest before you leave school.

Do you get to choose whether your loans are subsidized or unsubsidized? Not really. It depends on the level of education and the school. Again, reading the fine print on your loans and asking questions up front will provide you with the information you need. Remember, know the lay of the land! Each situation is different, and the more you know, the better your decision-making power will be.

Familiarize yourself with these definitions and they will help you better understand student loan debt. Still feeling uncertain or confused? There is more detailed information available on the Federal Student Aid website. This is a website that you should frequent to develop a working knowledge of the tools and resources they provide. I utilize this website at least monthly; I manage my information down to that level. Please, do your homework! Whose future is it? It's your future and you need to understand what resources, choices, and consequences are available to support your financial future.

There are also several other types of options to fund your education, some of which you are not required to pay back. These include:

- **Scholarships and Grants:** Congratulations if you have qualified for a scholarship or received grant money. This is free money!

Take advantage of it and make the most of your opportunity. Keep in mind that you might have to meet certain criteria if you do accept a scholarship or grant. For instance, when it comes to your Grade Point Average (GPA), you might have to maintain a minimum GPA to continue receiving the scholarship. If the GPA falls below the requirements, the scholarship could be taken away for a semester or all together. Again, read the fine print. According to a 2015 study by NerdScholar, the higher education team at NerdWallet, "High school graduates in the U.S. left more than $2.9 billion in free federal grant money unused over the last academic year." That's a lot of money left on the table that would have helped to address student loan debt and its epidemic. So, spend some time researching all of the possible scholarships. Trust me, it's worth it! Check out apps that are geared toward scholarships, such as Sholly, a personalized scholarship search app.

If you receive a teaching grant, keep in mind that there might be a requirement to teach a certain number of years under specific circumstances. If you do not meet the requirements, then the money could turn into a loan. Again, understand the details of what the offer is. You can find more information on these items by visiting the TEACH Grants section on the Federal Student Aid website.

- **Work-Study:** Basically, this program means that you have to work a part-time job while going to school. Work-study programs are administered by schools that participate in the Federal Work-Study Program. Check with your school's financial aid office to find out if your school participates. I can see many advantages by participating in this program; you are building your resume with work experience for the post-academic life (a.k.a. the real world) and you are learning time management skills. These are life skills that you can and will use the rest of your life. This is also a great talking point for your first interview. I agree that becoming an adult is awful, but we all have to do it. I have tremendous respect for anyone that goes to school and works a full-time or part-time job. It is an absolute challenge. If you don't believe me, ask someone who does it. I know students who have done everything from scooping ice cream in the cafeteria to working in the computer labs.

How you are paid depends partly on whether you're an undergraduate or graduate student (studentaid.ed.gov):

- If you are an undergraduate student, you're paid hourly.
- If you are a graduate or professional student, you're paid by the hour or by salary, depending on the work you do.

- Your school must pay you at least once a month.

Your school must pay you directly unless you request that the school:

- Send your payments directly to your bank account.
- Use the money to pay for your education-related institutional charges such as tuition, fees, and room and board.

Do. Your. Research! There are many options for scholarships and grants. I receive weekly emails from my current school with scholarship information. If you are interested in a certain career field, such as supply chain, human resources, or marketing, national societies might offer student scholarships as well. I know the Society of Human Resource Management (SHRM) does because I have received multiple scholarships from that organization. Below are a few online resources to scholarships and grants.

- Federal Student Aid: Grants Section
- ScholarshipsandGrants.us

Again, do your homework and make sure that the scholarships and grants are legitimate and not scams. Will it take work? Absolutely. While searching for scholarships is easier with apps and online access, applicants still need to write essays and gather recommendation letters. Who likes writing essays? People who want free money. Also, keep in mind that some scholarships can be taxable income. How do I know this? I learned the hard way when I paid a fine three years after receiving a scholarship! Read the fine print and know your responsibilities for each type of funding you receive. Again, know the lay of the land!

The fine print will vary based on the loan, scholarship, grant, and work-study program. The more questions you ask and research you do, the better your decision making will become. The fine print is drafted in a way to keep us from wanting to read it. Who reads the fine print when they register on a website or apply for a credit card? Not very many of us. However, reading the fine print for your student loans is very important. The fine print can and does determine your future financial health. As noted in an earlier section, I know that none of us want to be making payments on student loan debt when going into retirement. Read the fine print and ask questions if you have them. Allow yourself to be the expert.

SECTION 7

Plan of Attack

We all have to take responsibility for our actions and decisions, regardless of the situation it puts us in or the financial hardship it might end up causing. Fiscal responsibility varies from person to person and situation to situation. We all come from unique backgrounds and have differing responsibilities related to our situations. I personally live on a razor thin budget and have done so since 2011. The budget has gotten even tighter now that I have started my own business and am working on a second graduate degree. Do I *have* to do this? Nope. I *choose* to do it. We all make choices in life and we have to live with those choices, good or bad. Fiscal responsibility is one of those choices we need to make in order to live a debt-free life.

Analyze Your Debt

The first thing we all need to start with is prioritizing and understanding our current debt load. Is it important for us to live debt-free? My answer is a resounding yes. Again, I do not like to see the government or bankers making money off my debt. Living a debt-free life is my priority; therefore, repaying my student loans is a priority in my life.

Sit down and take a look at your debt. All of your debt, not just your student loans. Which debt has the highest interest rate? Review all of your accounts and understand what debt has the highest interest rate and set goals of paying that one off first. Do some research to find out if you can consolidate or refinance the debt to lower the interest rate.

After reviewing, think creatively about consolidation or refinancing. Can you do either of these with your current institutions? Do they offer an option for either of these? If not, can you transfer money to another bank? If you owe money on a credit card, can you transfer the balance to a new card with 0% interest for twelve months and set a goal to repay the entire amount in twelve months? What about a car note? Is there an option to refinance the car note at a lower rate? Does your employer offer a refinancing option if you utilize their credit union? Some employers will do this for employees. The idea is to organize your debts, reduce interest rates where you can, and possibly consolidate loans if it makes sense.

I have found when refinancing car notes, banks or credit unions are open to refinancing at a lower rate if you agree to repay the entire loan in less time. I recently received an offer to refinance my truck loan, but all the credit union could do was match the current interest rate. Yet they wanted the truck paid off in half the time! What sense does that make? Not very much. Do your homework regarding balance transfers and credit consolidation. We will cover student loan consolidation in an upcoming section.

Wants vs. Needs

When discussing financial responsibility, we need to define a need versus a want. This varies from person to person and situation to situation. It is a simple concept, but it takes extreme discipline to live by this simple concept because we live in an "I want it now" society. Do you really *need* a new cell phone...or do you just *want* one? Do you *need* a new car...or do you just *want* one? Do you *need* the best cable package with high speed internet...or do you just *want* it? Do you *need* new shoes...or do you just *want* them? See where I'm going with this?

I cannot define needs and wants for every person with student loan debt. That needs to be defined at an individual level. However, before each purchase, ask yourself, "Do I really *need* XYZ...or do I just *want* XYZ?"

Fiscal responsibility takes tremendous sacrifice, organization, and discipline. The skills and habits you develop in your becoming debt-free journey debt will serve you for the rest of your life. If we all evaluate purchases on a need versus want approach, we will live a financially healthier life.

Savings and 401k

What about savings? I think we should all have money in savings for a "what if" situation. The amount of money you put in savings is up to you. Some people have twelve months, six months and some live with just a month of savings in case of emergency. That will be based on your definition of risk. Are you willing to have less in savings for now while you focus on paying off your debt?

Keep in mind, savings accounts are generating almost 0% interest while your loans' interest rates will range between 4%-8%. (For student loans. Car loans and credit cards may be higher.)

If you work for an organization that offers a 401k match, take advantage of it, otherwise you are leaving free money on the table.

Fiscal responsibility is an acquired skill for most. We all need to live financially healthy lives. The choice is yours on how to approach fiscal responsibility. Living for the now will probably not get you to a debt-free future. If you need help working through the details, ask for help. Asking for help is never a bad thing; it shows that we care and want to take steps in living a debt-free future. Set goals and discuss them with a professional. Once you reach a milestone, reward yourself. Challenge yourself! I have no doubt with sacrifice and discipline we can all be student loan debt-free.

SECTION 8

How to Put Out the Fire: Diminish Your Debt

So. Much. Money. In the United States, we currently owe over $1.6 trillion in student loan debt. That means millions of Americans already have taken on large amounts of debt. Is it the end of the world as we know it? Absolutely not. You are on the path to living debt-free, and applying principles from this book is the first step to getting you there.

There's no magic formula to solve all of your student loan debt problems, but developing a framework or roadmap will start you on the path to success. Be strict, be focused, and be action-oriented. This outline below worked well for me, and my goal is that you will apply it to your current situation. Yes, bringing in a relatively high income helped, and yes, I lived on less than $1,000 per month. I was dedicated; this allowed me to pay off all the debt in a significantly reduced amount of time. Your goal should be to maximize your income while reducing your expenses.

At the time of finishing my first graduate degree, I accepted a job in northern Michigan in a town with a population under 15,000 and on average 20 degrees below zero in the winter. Rent on my two-bedroom house was $550 per month plus utilities. I had basic cable, with no high speed internet. I had a monthly cellphone bill, no car payment, no credit card debt and paid my insurance every six months. I had two other bills at the time; a monthly gym membership and groceries.

I cut out all the extra expenses that I did not need at the time. Fail to plan, plan to fail. I defined my version of need versus want. Do I need it, and will this purchase help me in achieving my goal? Consistency helped me stay on track, and my focus helped me achieve my goal.

As I was drafting the first edition of this book, I was in the process of planning fundamentally how and how quickly I could pay off the debt from my second master's degree in 2018. Yes, the time will go by fast and that money will be due before the ink is dry on the sheepskin, but I know I always have a game plan set in place.

In 2014, I wrote an article published by Business Insider on how I paid off almost $74,000 in student loans in less than 24 months. The article outlined 16 tips (below) that helped me in reaching my goal of being student loan debt-free. Was reaching that goal easy? Absolutely not. You have to be able to do things other people simply will not do. It takes tremendous sacrifice and discipline. If I can do it, so can you. I have no doubt everyone reading this book has the ability to set an achievable goal and then go out and reach it.

Follow these 16 tips. Create your own process and share it with others who will hold you accountable. Remember, I was and will be in the same situation as you again: up to my eyeballs in debt and figuring out the quickest process to pay it off. I hate owing money to anyone and refuse to sit on that amount of debt for 30 years. Here are the tips that helped me take immediate control of my financial future.

1. Don't Ignore the Debt

Let's face it, we know that the debt exists and eventually we will have to pay it back. Why ignore it? The best option is to be as proactive as possible and start the repayment process.

Ignoring the debt could make everything worse: compounding interest, ruined credit, wage garnishments, social security garnishments, and so on. You might ignore the debt, but the debt will never ignore you. As I wrote earlier in the book, people are employed to track us down when we do not pay our bills. Update your records and utilize technology for payments. If you need more time to make a payment, ask for it, but whatever you do, do not ignore the debt.

2. Read the Fine Print and Know the Repayment Guidelines

Learn from my mistakes. I will be the first one to admit that I did not read every detail of the loans I was taking out in graduate school. In fact, I owed $15,000 more than I had expected at the end of the program. That is a tremendous amount of additional money to owe on student loan debt, and it's not easy to repay. My advice remains consistent: understand the loans in painfully finite detail. Understand the repayment guidelines, the total amount due, what each payment goes toward (interest versus principal) who receives the payment, and so on. Most loan documents are the same—

to an extent—but terms, conditions, and rates will vary based on the loan type and issuing authority.

3. Be Prepared To Sacrifice In Order To Meet Your Goals

This is where strategy comes into play. Write down your budget (or use Excel or an app), after you define your needs versus wants. My own personal process was mentally taxing, and halfway through I questioned why and what I was doing. Was it worth it? Of course. Will it be worth it again? Time will tell. But, you have to decide what you are personally willing to sacrifice in order to reach your goal. What do you essentially need in order to survive while repaying the debt? Everyone's personal situation is different. I get it. But that doesn't mean we can't all make sacrifices in the short term to live debt-free long term.

Take a break here and spend some time working on and setting a realistic goal. Brainstorm areas that you can reign in on in order to live debt-free. How can you cut back on expenses? How can you add to your income? Dog walking? Lawn mowing? Sell stuff on Facebook Marketplace or

Craigslist? Be creative, but finding ways to increase your income will help to meet your goals.

I had no car payment, no internet bill, and no credit card debt. My outgoing funds went to rent, utilities, groceries, car insurance, and a cellphone bill. I lived on almost nothing; be prepared to do the same if you set a goal as extreme as mine. Anyone can do it, all it takes is sacrifice, persistence, and willpower.

4. Keep Your Contact Information Current

This tip is useful with all your responsibilities in life. Keep your information current in the debtor's system. Many people will utilize a college email account for any correspondence related to college, but within six months of graduation that email address could be turned off and your information is going into a black hole. You probably won't be living at the same address that you did in college either. It is your responsibility to update your information. Most organizations allow you to make all the necessary changes on their website, to ensure accuracy, and to make the process more efficient. Take ten minutes and review your accounts and addresses.

You don't need emails or actual mail going to where you can't receive them, especially when it involves your debt and what's due.

5. Make More Than Minimum Payments Every Chance You Get

I live by this tip in my life now. At the time I paid off my student loans, I was making triple or quadruple payments every month. Instead of paying the $650 minimum payment, I was paying $2,600 per month. Again, I understand not everyone can make payments on that level. But even paying $20, $30, or $50 extra every month will add up in the long run. If you get a tax refund or money from a relative at Christmas, use it to make a payment! Pay off the high interest stuff first: credit cards, vehicles, and then focus on the lower interest debt. Make a spreadsheet or use an app to track your progress because when you see that number depleting, you will be that much more motivated to send extra money toward it. Make it like a game if you have to. How much extra can you pay down in one, six, or twelve months? Then set up a game plan to do it.

6. Start Paying Immediately

The grace period to begin repayment is generally six months then the process begins, and that clock will tick every month. Under certain circumstances the grace period can be extended to twelve months. If you—like many other people—received money for graduation from friends and relatives or a sign-on bonus for a new job, why not use the money to make a payment? Just because the paperwork states six months does not mean by any stretch of the imagination that you need to wait six months before starting to pay. If you can make payments before you graduate, do it. The sooner you start, the sooner you will be debt-free. I graduated in December 2011 and made my first payment in February 2012. Even then, I had no reason to wait. All waiting does is build more and more interest on top of the debt. Why let others make money off of your debt through accruing interest?

7. Pay More Than Once Per Month If Possible

In recent positions, I received a monthly paycheck. For anyone who has never worked for a place that pays monthly, rest assured that learning to budget around a once a month check is a painful learning process. My paycheck was deposited into my account on the last working day of the month, I made sure to get up and pay every bill that morning before going to work and to leave money in my account for the rest of the month. Throughout the month, I made small payments here and there on my student loans. These smaller amounts, because they went toward the principal, kept the interest from accruing and kept me on course to achieve my goal.

Again, if you have $20, $30, or $40 extra during the month, make a payment! In some months, I made five or six separate payments. It's better to make several small payments when the funds are available than it is to try and save up during the entire month to make an extra payment, as that money might end up going to something frivolous instead. Remember, a few swipes on your phone can send a quick payment—just make sure to identify it as going toward the principal. You'll see how quickly the principal goes down, saving you on interest payments.

8. Live Well Below your Means

This tip comes back to knowing the difference between a want and a need. Do you need it—or do you just want it? This can be a complete life change in a society that is defined by instant gratification. Learn what your needs are and start cutting away the excess. Figure out what your limits are. These are long-lasting life choices. The only way I can survive in graduate school now is through the discipline I instilled through my first journey. Every journey begins with the first step, and moving slowly is still considered making progress. Rather than feeling overwhelmed, allow yourself to be excited when you drop that loan down by another $100 or $1,000.

9. Set a Strict Cash Budget

I make cash purchases for almost everything except for gas, cellphone, insurance, gym membership, and Internet. I withdraw a set amount of cash each week and track my purchases closely. At the time of my repayment, I only withdrew $40 per week for my expenses. Using cash has its advantages and disadvantages. The advantage is that when it's gone, it's gone. The disadvantage is that it takes discipline to track what you purchase with cash.

Again, it helps to learn how to budget and track expenses in a spreadsheet, a cell phone app, or a tool on the Internet. Budgeting tools are available for free; I use a basic spreadsheet to track everything and reconcile against my bank accounts. Again, know your expenses and what you can sacrifice. Do you really need a $5 cup of coffee in the morning or do you just want it? I agree, I want it too! And, if I have an extra $5 at the end of the week, I might just treat myself to it.

10. Pay Off the Highest Interest Loans First

Pay off the high interest account balances first. In my experience, credit cards will have a significantly higher interest rate than a student loan. If you use a credit card, pay it off at the end of the month. I use credit cards all the time, but I haven't paid a dime in interest since 2010. I actually take complete advantage of the rewards and points without paying the credit card companies any interest. Paying off credit card or other high interest debt will save you money that can be put towards living a debt-free life. Once you get the high interest loans paid off, close any unnecessary accounts or credit cards. I have yet to figure out why people in the United States need 15 credit cards. I have two credit cards, neither of which carry any balance. Do you need 15 credit cards, or do you want 15 credit cards?

11. Don't Buy a New Car if You Don't Need One

I went against my own advice when I decided to buy a brand-new truck. Did I need it? Nope, I wanted it and I wanted it right then. See, we all make mistakes and mine will cost me about $45,000 plus interest. Don't get me wrong, I love the truck, but it wasn't a necessity, it was a want. That's what marketing professionals call an "impulse buy". The dealer didn't even have to sell it to me. I just walked in and bought it. I know that made his day, and hopefully he spent the commission money on paying off some of his own debt!

Anyway, if you have a vehicle that is paid for and requires minimal maintenance and upkeep, keep it for a few years. The money you save on a new car payment and increased insurance costs, can be used as additional payments towards student loans and any other debt. Again, understand the need versus want. Do you need a new car, or do you want a new car? I wanted a new truck and I bought one! Now I have a large monthly payment until the truck note is paid in full. On average, I drive my vehicles for eight years, but now I'm hoping the truck will last a decade so I can drive it debt-free for a long time.

12. Look for Cheaper Places to Live While you are Paying Down Debt

We all define location differently. Many of us want to work in New York, Chicago, Seattle, or Los Angeles, all of which are great cities with great people. But guess what? The cost of living there will be two to three times as much as other places. I chose to work in Escanaba, Michigan—of all places—for two years because of the high salary and low cost of living. I knew the sacrifice back then would pay off in the future. I encourage you to look for those unique places to live for a few years. You might fall in love with the location and live there forever. If not, set a goal and plan your exit strategy. You will benefit by repaying more student loan debt and gaining great experience for your resume that could lead to an even better future position.

13. Learn to Negotiate

Negotiating salaries, sign-on bonuses, relocations, and other perks have been a true advantage to me over the past several years. When I left graduate school, I had two competing offers. I leveraged one offer against the other, which led to a higher salary, better relocation money, and an increased sign-on bonus. Every dollar of that money went directly to my student loan repayment. Negotiation is a skill that all of us need to acquire because almost everything in life comes down to negotiations. Never leave money on the table. There are plenty of books and articles on salary and benefit negotiation. Don't be afraid to ask questions or point out additional benefits that you bring to the table. What's the worst they can do? Tell you no! But, what if they say yes?

14. Track your Payments Closely

I take time on a daily basis to look at my accounts on each of my lender's websites. When I make payments, I review the account the following day to ensure that everything was processed and updated correctly. I track my payments down to the penny. Can mistakes happen? Of course. I overpaid my final payment by 18 cents, and it still took me six months to get the money back. I wasn't particularly concerned about the 18 cents, but I was concerned about the account remaining open in the system and on my credit report. When you make a final payment on an account, make sure it closes out and get the fact that it's closed in writing. After a few months, make sure that that account is closed on your credit report.

15. Take Advantage of Discounts

I have received discounts for signing up for automatic monthly withdrawals from my checking account. My advice is once again to research the institution and understand discounts that may be applied to your debt. A savings of 0.25% adds up over the life of the loan. I signed up immediately and began making payments. If your institution doesn't offer a discount, find one that does via consolidation.

16. Set Achievable Milestones, and Reward Yourself as You Reach Them

I have yet to fully master this last tip. I paid off all of my student loan debt and then decided to buy a new $45,000 truck and to take out $100,000 more in student loan debt. I am a glutton for punishment, and I love student loan debt. However, I also love paying it off.

I do not sleep well knowing that the government and banks are making money off my debt. That was my motivation for paying back the money in 23 months. I literally checked the website daily and watched the interest accrue. After seven days, it went up one-hundred dollars (at the peak of my debt). It made me sick watching that number increase and it should not sit well with you either, watching your debt grow through interest.

Take it day by day. Develop a process and be disciplined enough to try it for six months. If it does not work, revise it and try something different. You have to understand what all your money is being spent on and where it is going. Cash transactions make it extremely challenging to manage your money exactly.

As you work on your own budget and towards your goals, set mini-goals with rewards. Take a few minutes and set a goal. Write it down and carry it with you. Tell people about it. The more you talk about the goal, the more accountable you will be to yourself in achieving the goals that you set. Just thinking about it or wishing it will not make it happen. If you pay off a credit card or a high interest student loan account, reward yourself with a nice dinner or weekend trip. I am not suggesting a trip to Hawaii or a month-long journey to Europe, just something to remind yourself as to why you are willing to do what others are not. The milestones will help you build momentum in achieving your ultimate goal of living a debt-free life.

Now that I own a small consulting business, I track everything down to the penny. This was a complete change from what I was accustomed to. Previously, I had a broad sense of how I spent money, but now I truly know my finances inside and out. If I didn't know my finances to this level, it would only cost me more when my accountant asks for information. Being on top of my accounts and balances saves me from paying them to figure out things I should already know.

Make Your Customized Budget and Plan

Take the time to review your personal finances and develop a plan to attack that debt head-on. The Excel document I use for my budget contains multiple sheets outlining the below-mentioned information. You may want to use an app or other method, but as long as it's easy for you to understand and maintain, use what works best for you.

Here's where to start:

- Gather all of your accounts, bills, and bank statements.
- Write down—or plug into an app or Excel spreadsheet—each of your debts and break them down by minimum monthly payments and interest rates.
- Write down all the payments you make every month including mortgages, rent, student

loans, vehicles, transportation, credit cards, cellphones, cable bill, insurance, tuition, Internet, gym membership, groceries, and utilities.

- Note your net income (take home) per month.

If your income fluctuates, use an average, but you'll need to adjust each month. When your income is above your average, guess what? You guessed it! Send that payment to your loans. Once you've gathered the data, find a reputable financial planner or credit counselor and schedule an appointment. If your income and debt is pretty manageable and you have an economically savvy family member or friend, ask them to help you review your plan or even build the plan from the ground up. Develop a process that works for you and hold yourself accountable to review and update weekly. Know that nothing will change unless you want it to change, and think of this as a living document. It can and should be tweaked and updated as your lifestyle changes. The process only works if you remain disciplined and are willing to engage. From there, it is up to you to make the detailed plan, work the plan, and modify the plan. If you don't do it, who else will?

I have repeated myself a few times in this book, with a purpose. The purpose is practice makes improvement. The more you practice and discipline yourself in this process, the more success you will find. Success doesn't happen overnight for anyone. It takes determination, sacrifice, and in many cases, failure to find success. We all fail, it isn't the end of the world. It's a lesson on where you can improve and what you need to change.

I spend a lot of time researching ways to repay student loan debt, along with the questions people have and the extremes people will go to in order to become debt-free. The websites below have helpful hints, checklists, and frequently asked questions for anyone just starting the process of repaying their student loans. There are also calculators and other tools to help you get started. If these websites don't work for you personally, then research additional alternatives. Microsoft Excel offers basic budgeting templates; you can build your own. I agree reading some of this stuff is frustrating and discouraging, but you must invest time to develop a process that will help you become debt-free. If you won't take the time to understand it, who will? It is your life and you make the choice to drown in debt or swim in success.

- Federal Student Aid: Student Loan Repayment
- Federal Student Aid: Loan Repayment Checklist
- Federal Student Aid: Repayment Plans

My closing thought in this section is to ensure you have all of your records updated. Keep your phone number, address, email, and other information updated in the debtor's systems so there is no confusion regarding payment processing. Know what bills must be paid when. If possible, have the payments directly withdrawn from your checking or savings account. Again, this will save you time and streamline the process. You will not miss the money if it is already gone!

The real difficulty is getting started. Pay off the high interest debt first and know the difference between a want and a need. These are decisions we all must make in life. It is not easy to stay disciplined when everyone else has nicer equipment, a better car, nicer clothes, and so on. I used a BlackBerry Storm for three years while I was paying off my student loan debt. Remember BlackBerry? Again, I could go out and buy a nicer phone, but I didn't want to spend the money. A need and/or a want will vary based on each individual situation.

A Note About Medical Debt

Because I haven't had to deal with medical debt, I reached out to my friend Jennifer who is sharing her experience with implications of healthcare on student loans:

Having a healthcare plan (be it public or private) does not make student loan borrowers less at risk of having to choose between making a student loan payment or paying for healthcare. I recently underwent a hernia surgery; I did not qualify for hospital subsidy because my income was over their threshold. I have a decent paying job, where I have health benefits that are supposedly "good". The insurance is structured in such a way that I need to pay the entire deductible before a co-pay goes into effect. For me, this means that I needed to pay $6,500 out of pocket for the surgery, before I received any assistance from my health insurance. Thankfully, I was able to negotiate a payment plan with the hospital. However, I had some choices to make; if I were to not make a payment to the hospital, they could refuse services, which means that I would not be provided post-surgical medical care. If I forego post-surgical care, and let the bill go to collections, the impact to my overall credit could be detrimental to my future financial stability.

Deciding to pay medical bills means that I need to cut costs elsewhere. Knowing that my most sizable expenditure is my school loans. I called the loan company, explaining my situation and asked if I could get a lower payment. My "lower" payment was about $650, down from $800, but still too much for one income to sustain while also making $600 payments to the hospital. My only other option was forbearance for a year; I chose forbearance.

This isn't an isolated event, at the beginning of each year, my medicine cost the same as one of my paychecks. Even if I were to live frugally, as suggested in this book, I still wouldn't be able to pay for my basic needs, my healthcare costs, and my school loans simultaneously. This will be a perpetual cycle of needing forbearance or deferment and amassing interest, adding to my overwhelming debt.

I know that I am not alone in being put in a position of having to choose. As our generation ages, the need for medical procedures and medicine will increase. Putting loans in forbearance or deferment will cause those original 20 year student loans to easily turn into 35 years.

SECTION 9

Forbearance or Deferment: That is the Question

As graduation becomes a closer reality, so does the harsh reality of student loan payments. For many with private student loans, there is no other option but to buckle down and start chipping away at the debt, payment after payment. For those with federal student loans, there are two different options to consider when hitting the pause button - deferment and forbearance. In order to qualify for either one, you must be up to date on your loans.

Deferment vs Forbearance

Deferment and forbearance are similar in that they both allow you to postpone your monthly federal student loan payments. Yet, they are different in very important ways, so it's important to know the differences.

Deferment

This is the process that most of us follow when we are in school. Deferring loans is a period of time in which repayment of the principal and interest is temporarily delayed. As you work towards a degree and you take out loans as a freshman, in most cases loan payments will not be due for six months after graduation or six months after you stop going to school. Remember: you must repay the borrowed money even if you never finish school.

How do we become eligible for deferment?

- Full-time or part-time college enrollment.
- During a period of unemployment or inability to find a full-time job. We can defer for up to three years during this period. However, I know hundreds of people with student loan debt and none of which have qualified for a three-year deferral.
- Economic hardship. We can defer for up to three years with this option as well. This includes participating in Peace Corps services.
- Active military or returning from active service in the military.

Deferring payments means you are postponing your monthly payments on subsidized federal loans without accruing interest. You also don't have to pay interest on the subsidized portion of direct consolidation loans or FFEL Consolidation Loans during deferment. Be careful if your loans are unsubsidized- a deferment allows you to postpone payments but the interest will continue to accrue during the deferment period. You have the option to pay the interest portion during your deferment period in order to avoid having it capitalized, or added to your principal, but that is not required.

To receive a deferment, you must apply directly to your loan servicer. For information on how to contact your loan servicer, you can check the National Student Loan Data System. Deferments are typically granted in six-month increments.

Forbearance

Forbearance might be a good option for those who don't qualify for deferment. If you or I cannot make our scheduled loan payment and in the unfortunate event that we do not qualify for deferment, we might have the option of forbearance. If approved, forbearance will allow us to stop or reduce payments for up to twelve months. What is the disadvantage? People will still make money off of your debt as the interest will continue to accrue on subsidized or unsubsidized loans, including all PLUS loans. That accrued interest will be capitalized, or added to your balance, unless you pay the interest during the forbearance period.

Types of Forbearance

Mandatory forbearance is granted regardless of whether or not the lender agrees with your eligibility. There are some situations where forbearance is mandatory, meaning your loan servicer is required to offer you forbearance. If you qualify for mandatory forbearance it is granted. You can acquire this if:

- You are working in a medical or dental internship or residency program.
- The total amount owed each month for all student loans received is 20% or more of your total monthly gross income. This looks like a great option for anyone with a large amount of student loan debt, but hold on. Additional

conditions will apply. Again read the fine print.
- You have served in a national service position and have been awarded.
- You are a teacher and qualify for teacher loan forgiveness.
- You qualify for partial repayment of your loans under the U.S. Department of Defense Student Loan Repayment Program.
- You are a member of the National Guard and have been activated by a governor, but you are not eligible for military deferment.

Discretionary forbearance is decided by the lender or organization that you owe money to. They decided whether to grant forbearance; based upon reasons such as the borrower's financial hardship, medical expenses or a change in work situation.

Should you apply for deferment or forbearance?

Based on your personal situation, you'll need to understand which option is right for you. Here are some helpful questions to ask yourself before applying for either:

- Is my current financial situation temporary? Something like a job loss or long-term illness can undoubtedly make your financial future unpredictable. But if you're confident you'll get things under control within a certain time frame, then deferment or forbearance could be a good option for you.
- Do I qualify for deferment or forbearance? Before making the decision to pursue either repayment option, you'll need to make sure you meet the specific criteria required to qualify. As previously mentioned, factors such as the type of loan, your specific financial hardship and other circumstances will be considered.
- Is postponing my student loan payments an absolute must? If you can find a way to simply restructure your budget and/or adjust your current repayment schedule, it could be a much simpler way to get a handle on your student loan debt than applying for deferment or forbearance.

If you do decide to apply, understanding the differences between deferment vs. forbearance is an important part of being an informed borrower. Whether or not you are currently facing an economic hurdle, the ability to pause student loan payments is one of the biggest perks of federal student loans.

How to apply for forbearance vs. deferment

If you need to pause your payments through either deferment or forbearance, even if the reason is a mandatory one, you still have to apply because the process is not an automatic one.

You will likely be required to submit documentation to support your request and demonstrate that you meet the eligibility requirements. Once you submit your request for deferment or forbearance, continue to pay your monthly payments until you know if your request has been granted. If you fail to make payments, and your deferment or forbearance request is denied, then you will be considered delinquent and will risk defaulting on your loan. That is not a situation you want to be in.

Grace Period

Both forbearance and deferment offer you a grace period. A grace period is defined as a period in which you will not have to make payments on the amount of money you owe in student loan debt. During a grace period, interest will still continue to accrue on the already owed amount. Grace periods are valuable for people in transition and provides additional time to make necessary adjustments to budgets to pay back debt. Grace periods will vary in length between forbearance and deferment. Generally, the grace period after graduation or leaving school is six months.

Know That The Choice Is Yours

These options were designed to assist all of us in making the best choices for each of our unique situations. There are programs out there for all of us, and researching and understanding these programs will help you make the best possible decision. If you don't ask or don't know, how can you make a sound choice? Deferring is easy if you continue your education. Just remember that the interest will accrue, and lenders make money off your accruing interest. Research and review all options for your situation. You might save money over the life of the debt. Remember deferment and forbearance can have different meanings, but default is not a place any of us want to be.

SECTION 10

Uniting the Kingdoms: Student Loan Consolidation

You can sense the gimmick from a mile away- the big statements and questions trying to evoke a sense of fear and urgency. I see many television advertisements pitching student loan debt consolidation, but I have no trust in advertisements like that. Some of my close friends have consolidated loans and are happy with the results. They worked out the paperwork and application submission on their own. I suggest that you review your options and choose one that suits your financial and lifestyle needs.

Beware of Sharks

There are businesses that offer consolidation services, and this option has turned into a very lucrative business. These businesses fill out the application to consolidate for you, which can cost on average seven hundred dollars per application. The ads that I see on TV are targeting fear and complexity. They target the fear of the unknown and the concept that only professionals are qualified to fill out these applications due to the complex submission process. Keep in mind that these individuals are trained *salespeople*. Any good salesperson will close a deal and land the sale. If you are concerned about the process and filing the paperwork, research a few consolidation companies and gather price quotes. Once you are in their system, the likelihood is that phone call after phone call will start. I will admit that some of the offers look good, especially comparing interest rates. However, my concern is the upfront costs to be approved or denied consolidation.

My recommendation is simple: know your options. They will depend on your current financial situation, future financial situation, and level of student loan debt. If you feel comfortable consolidating the loans and submitting the application, why not try it? What's the worst they can do? Tell you no! If you are considering hiring a consolidation company to fill out the application for you, think twice. That $700 can be put toward student loan debt or you could pay down another form of debt.

If the forms are confusing, ask for assistance from a financial advisor, trusted banker, or a friend or relative who understands the forms. There are plenty of people out there who have gone through the process before who will probably help you for free. If you don't ask, you'll never know. Our goal is to keep spending at a minimum, and that $700 can be used in other, more proactive ways.

Meeting the Criteria

There are several loans that are eligible for loan consolidation. You must meet certain criteria and those criteria will vary based on the loan type and financial situation of the individual requesting consolidation. Eligible loans include direct subsidized, direct unsubsidized, subsidized federal Stafford loans, unsubsidized federal Stafford loans, direct PLUS loans, PLUS loans from the Federal Family Education Loan (FFEL) program, supplemental loans for students, federal Perkins loans, federal nursing loans, health education assistance loans, and *some* existing consolidation loans. If you have existing loans that have been consolidated, you might be able to consolidate again with new loans.

Private loans are not eligible for consolidation. These loans are owned by a private bank and the fine print is different. Understanding your loan and loan types continues to be important before, during, and after completion of degree. It can and does impact your future.

We have discussed student loans for student borrowers in detail. PLUS loans are taken out by a parent; they impact a parent's credit and will remain the responsibility of the parent over the life of the loan. A student cannot apply for loan consolidation and consolidate the PLUS loan from the parents into that consolidation application. If you are a parent, this might sound disappointing. However, parents can apply to consolidate the PLUS loans themselves. Just remember that the responsibility will still remain with you over the life of the loan.

Qualifying for consolidation requires that you have at least one Direct Loan or FFEL Program loan that is in a grace period or in the process of repayment. Most students or parents will have more than one loan when they go through an academic program from start to finish. If any of these loans are in default, the consolidation process becomes more complex and certain requirements must be met before an applicant can be considered for consolidation. Everyone's situation is different. The more you understand about your loans the better your decision making process will be and future financial freedom.

The last thing the federal government or a private bank wants is for anyone to stop paying on their debt. I cannot see any advantage to them, besides a write-off of bad debt at the end of the year. Again, my friends have been successful with loan consolidation, but they did the work on their own and did not pay a third party to apply for them.

Let's face it: we owe the money. If someone owed you money, my guess is you would want to be paid back as well. They want to be paid and are willing to work with all of us if we meet certain criteria. Research all your options and make a choice that works best for your personal situation. You never know until you ask.

SECTION 11

The Impossible Quest: Cancellation or Discharge

There are options out there for individuals with student loan debt. It is up to us to research and utilize the tools and resources available to us. If you don't do it, who else will?

The truth of the matter is that student loan debt is nearly impossible to have cancelled or discharged. Let's focus on how to strategically approach the process. If you do qualify for cancellation or discharge, your options are to fill out the application yourself or to ask for assistance. If someone is taking time to work through the process with you, show your appreciation and take them to lunch or dinner to talk it over. Once again, there are companies that will fill the necessary paperwork out for you for a hefty fee, but you can probably live without them.

Is it worth your time to review the information if you think you might qualify for some amount of your loans being discharged? Absolutely!

The information provided below is for federal loans. Here are typical situations where debt can be cancelled or discharged:

- **Borrower's total and permanent disability or death** - My assumption is that in the unfortunate event that you passed away, you probably won't be reading this book and you will not have to pay your student loan debt. The debt in full will be discharged. If a parent borrowed on a PLUS loan and they pass away or if the student dies, the loan can also be discharged.
- **Bankruptcy** - In very rare circumstances, the court has ruled that student loans can be discharged due to bankruptcy. The individual must prove an undue hardship based on the Brunner Test.
- **School closures** - If a school closes prior to that individual finishing the program, the loans can be discharged. In recent news stories, there have been several for-profit school closures where this applies.

- **A false loan certification** - If the school falsely certifies a student's eligibility to receive a loan, this amount can also be discharged.
- **Identity theft** - If a student loan was granted due to identity theft, the person whose identity was stolen can have the loan amounts discharged.
- **A full-time teaching job for five consecutive years in an area defined as low-income** - This only applies to elementary or secondary schools. Certain criteria, such as poverty level in the school district, must be met to qualify for the discharge of the loans.
- **Loan forgiveness for public sector employees** - Borrowers must make payments for 120 consecutive months prior to applying for loan forgiveness with this option. Minimum payments must be made for a decade before applying for this loan forgiveness option.
- **Military service** - This requires hostile fire or imminent danger pay. Again, certain criteria must be met to qualify for the partial or full discharge of debt.

- **Public service** - Full-time firefighters, law enforcement officers, corrections officers, or, in some situations, nurses or medical technicians, can qualify for 100% discharge of loan debt.
- **VISTA or Peace Corps** - Volunteers can qualify for 70% of the student loan debt being discharged.
- **Specific employment situations**
    - A librarian with a Master's degree working in a Title I-eligible elementary or secondary school or in a public library serving Title I-eligible schools can qualify for up to 100% discharge.
    - A full-time attorney working in the federal public or community defender organization can qualify for up to 100% discharge.
    - A full-time employee of a public or nonprofit child or family service agency for high-risk children and their families from low-income communities can qualify for up to 100%.

- A full-time staff member in the education component of a Head Start program qualifies for up to 100%.
- A full-time qualified professional providers of early intervention services for the disabled qualifies for 100%
- Full-time special education teachers, speech pathologists, and bilingual educators can qualify for up to 100% discharge. Certain requirements must be met prior to discharging loans.
- A full-time faculty member at a tribal college or university qualifies up to 100%.

If you believe you do qualify for cancellation or discharge, why not apply? As I tell my students and friends about applying for jobs, "What's the worst they can do?" You will never know unless you try. Private lenders will have different rules and regulations regarding cancellation or discharge. Yes, it is probably contained in all that fine print that none of us like to read, but read all the information thoroughly and keep up on it.

Credit card companies change interest rates and repayment terms at times. The same thing can happen with student loan repayment terms, rates, processes, etc. This is your financial future, so take the time to understand your student loans. It isn't enjoyable, but it is necessary. Know your loan documents like the back of your hand and get into the habit of monitoring changes weekly.

SECTION 12

Banish Bankruptcy

One of the assignments during my MBA program was to write a legal research paper. I chose to write about student loans being discharged during the bankruptcy process. I found two cases in which all or a portion of student loan debt was discharged during a bankruptcy hearing. The legal brief below is written as a case study and examines the difficulty of discharging student loans during the bankruptcy process in a court of law. I did add an additional case focused on a student suing a law school for falsifying employment statistics and post-graduation employment success rates. It reinforces the court's stance on this issue, and also all of the angles people have tried to take to get their student loan debt written off. Courts have been saying no since the 1980s, and this is something I can't see them changing their stance on at all. Be sure to monitor and watch for any changes that the Circuit Courts may make, though unlikely, still important.

The objective of the assignment was to research a current case (the first listed below) and find other cases for and against the legal case and draft a conclusion to the case after arguing both sides. All cases involve the "Brunner Test", which is a test developed in the 1980s to define undue hardship related to student loan debt. Student loan debt has changed a lot since the 1980s, but the test is still exactly the same.

LEGAL CASE:

First Circuit Court of Appeals

Robert E. Murphy (Debtor) v. U.S. Department of Education Educational Credit Management Corporation (Other interested parties include Sallie Mae and College Board)

FACTS OF CASE:

In the United States, we currently have over $1.4 trillion in outstanding student loan debt. Mr. Robert Murphy signed for the federal PLUS loans (student loans taken out by parents to pay their childrens' college costs), and after going into a large amount of student loan debt, he lost his position as President of a manufacturing firm. As of October 2015, Mr. Murphy now age 65, has been unemployed for 13 years, stating that he is too old to find comparable employment and is over qualified for lower-paying jobs in his field. Mr. Murphy and his wife live on a very modest income of $15,000 a year, which his wife earns from working as a Teacher's Aide. Due to the modest income, Mr. Murphy is unable to make payments on the PLUS loans taken out for his childrens' education. Mr. Murphy now owes almost a quarter of a million dollars due to lack of payment and accumulated interest on the PLUS loans.

Mr. Murphy filed for bankruptcy, seeking relief for the PLUS student loans, and the bankruptcy court refused to discharge the debt, under the "Brunner Rule of Law." Mr. Murphy is currently acting as his own attorney and has appealed to the First Circuit Court of Appeals, arguing that the "Brunner Test" should be abandoned as related to "Undue Hardship" for insolvent debtors to be forced to repay their student loans as a parent borrower.

LEGAL BACKGROUND OF DISPUTE (ISSUE):

Under the current laws and regulations of the "Brunner Test" in the United States, individuals who are currently burdened with any amount of student loan debt are unable to discharge the debt during a bankruptcy hearing; except as discussed below in rare cases. The majority of individuals must meet one of the following criteria in order to discharge student loan debt; "closed school discharge, total and permanent disability discharge, death discharge, false certification of student eligibility or unauthorized payment discharge, unpaid refund discharge, teaching loan forgiveness, public service loan forgiveness, and borrower defense discharge".

Mr. Murphy is attempting to persuade the First Circuit Court of Appeals that the 1987 ruling in Marie Brunner v. New York State Higher Education Services Corp. should be abandoned for being too harsh in his situation as a parent borrower and considering his current financial status. The "Brunner Test" has almost 30 years of precedent and is currently used by many courts to define "Undue Hardship" for insolvent debtors in the repayment of student loan debt. "The district court adopted a standard for "Undue Hardship" requiring a three-part showing: (1) that the debtor cannot maintain, based on current income and expenses, a "minimal" standard of living for herself and her dependents and her dependents is forced to repay the loans; (2) that additional circumstances exist indicating that this state of affairs is likely to persist for a significant position of the repayment period of the student loans; and (3) that the debtor has made good faith efforts to repay the loans".

In summary, Mr. Murphy acting as his own legal council will try and convince the court that the current rules under the "Brunner "Undue Hardship" Test" is too harsh and that the student loan debt should be discharged.

LEGAL ISSUE OF CASE:

The legal issue in this case as seen in other cases is whether the student loan debt can be discharged in a bankruptcy proceeding, due to "Undue Hardship" that the student loan debt has caused and the individual is unable to repay any amount of student loan debt. The court system(s) have been reluctant to discharge (only on rare occasions) student loan debt in bankruptcy court or in any other court of law in the United States due to "Undue Hardship," under the current "Brunner Rule of Law." Mr. Murphy and other interested parties who have submitted briefs in support of Mr. Murphy have stated that the "Brunner Test" no longer makes sense as the test was written in 1987, prior to tuition costs and loan debt ballooning to $1.4 trillion.

In summary, the legal issue of the case is whether or not student loan debt signed by a parent (PLUS Loan) or the student is dischargeable under current bankruptcy law, in bankruptcy court, or any other court during the appeals process in the United States and the definition of "Undue Hardship" under the "Brunner Test."

RELEVANT RULES OF LAW (RULE OF LAW):

The relevant rule of law is the three-part "Brunner Test" determined in a 1987 "Marie Brunner v. New York State Higher Education Services Corp." court case and the definition of "Undue Hardship."

ANALYSIS:

Mr. Murphy will argue in an October of 2012 ruling by the United States Bankruptcy Appellate Panel of the Eighth Circuit, Susan M. Shaffer v. United States Department of Education, the court affirmed the bankruptcy court's ruling that student loans could be discharged, because they created an "Undue Hardship" for the individual who obtained the educational loans. Ms. Schaffer at the time had over $200,000 in student loan debt from multiple institutions of higher learning, never completing a degree program.

Mr. Murphy will also argue in a March of 2016 ruling by the United States Bankruptcy Court Eastern District of New York, Lesley Campbell vs. CitiBank, N.A., The Student Loan Corporation, Two Square Financial, Inc., CACH, LLC, and First Step Group, LLC, the court ruled in favor of the plaintiff (Ms. Campbell) discharging a portion of her student loans related to expenses incurred when studying and taking the bar exam, as the money owed created "Undue Hardship". The discharged amount was $15,000, currently Ms. Campbell owes close to $300,000 in total student loan expenses for law school and at the time was currently on repayment.

The U.S. Department of Education will argue in January of 2016, the Supreme Court turned down an appeal by Mark Tetzlaff attempting to have his $260,000 in student loan debt for business and law school discharged in bankruptcy court.

The United States Court of Appeals for the Seventh Circuit affirmed a ruling in Mark Warren Tetzlaff v. Educational Credit Management Corporation, that the bankruptcy court did not error and Mr. Tetzlaff had not made a good faith effort to pay his student loan debt. The U.S. Department of Education will also reference re Gerhardt in a 2003 ruling, Jonathon Gerhardt owed $77,000 in student loan debt and filed for bankruptcy after attending multiple institutions of higher learning. At the time, Mr. Gerhardt had paid a total of $755 on the outstanding student loan debt. The Court of Appeals for the First Circuit struck down the "Undue Hardship" claim by Mr. Gerhardt, holding the debt could not be discharged as Mr. Gerhardt had not met the current "Brunner Test" guidelines, by making a "Good Faith Effort" for repayment of the debt.

The final case the U.S. Department of Education will reference is a March of 2016 case where the jury in a 9-3 verdict, ruled in favor of Thomas Jefferson School of Law in the Alaburda v. Thomas Jefferson School of Law. In this case, Ms. Alaburda sued the law school for all of her student loan debt ($150,000) over fraudulent and misleading employment statistics, claiming that over 80% of graduates are employed upon graduation. Ms. Alaburda was a 2008 honors graduate from Thomas Jefferson School of Law in California and was unsuccessful at obtaining legal employment upon graduation, applying to many law firms. In referencing the case, it is not specifically related to bankruptcy proceedings, however, it provides more evidence of the court system's reluctance to grant relief on student loan debt in legal proceedings or cases related to financial bankruptcy.

LEGAL CONCLUSION:

The "Brunner Test" was set as precedent at a time when student loan debt was manageable and had not ballooned into an almost $1.5 trillion problem in the United States. The language in the precedent is almost 30 years old, and should be reviewed as related to current student debt issues and the definition under the test of "Undue Hardship."

Mr. Robert Murphy owes in excess of $200,000 in PLUS student loan debt, not for his own educational debt, but his children's. As the courts have consistently followed the

"Brunner Test" as precedent (except in very rare situations) in the past and defined "Undue Hardship", I do believe the court will rule in favor of the U.S. Department of Education and the student loan debt will not be discharged. I do believe the amount of student loan debt does create an "Undue Hardship" by definition on Mr. Murphy and his wife, but the courts have been consistent on interpretation of the law. However, the court must also consider if Mr. Murphy at the time of employment was making payments on the debt and made "Good Faith Effort" in paying down the loans.

As we approach $1.5 trillion in student loan debt, the student loan bankruptcy debate will continue to become a topic in the media, as education will become the biggest expense many people will incur in their lifetime. The "Brunner Test" as currently defined needs to be redefined in relation to ballooning higher education costs. Presidential candidates have indicated new systems for student loan debt relief however; change has not happened and the court system(s) continue to deny rule against individuals with student loan debt". (Burr, MBC 643, Syracuse University, June 2016).

Failing For-Profits

As the current laws continue to be interpreted, and the amount of interest the government is making off of student loan debt grows, it is unlikely that a bankruptcy court, court of appeals, or the Supreme Court will allow for the discharge of student loan debt during the bankruptcy process. While the courts have recently discharged student loan debt, the debt being discharged was due to for-profit institutions that had gone bankrupt. For instance, in the case of ITT Technical Institute. When this institution went bankrupt, it left the students and former students with a worthless degree or even a half-finished degree. Students had no chance to transfer credits to non-profit credentialed institutions. While I think the "Brunner Test" is outdated, that does not dismiss the fact that we all signed on the dotted line and accepted the educational loans. Why should taxpayers foot the bill for anyone's student loan mess?

As I wrote the first edition of this book, it was unlikely that you or I would be capable of discharging student loans through a bankruptcy process. This hasn't changed in the writing of the second edition either. It could potentially change someday, even though it has not since the mid-1980s with few exceptions. Some of the candidates for the 2020 election believe college should be free and there has been some talk of dismissing student loan debt. How that impacts repaying of loans is yet to be seen.

Research the cases and understand the process to know if this might apply to you. As a follow-up to the Murphy Case, the U.S. First Court of Appeals agreed with Murphy on the "Undue Hardship" argument and has since sent the settlement agreement to the bankruptcy court. There was no final decision in the case as of January 2017. Therefore, the loans were still outstanding at that time. If you're choosing to utilize student loans to fund your education, remember what you signed up for. Applying for bankruptcy doesn't just wipe them all away; it isn't free money. Take control of your financial situation and make smart decisions. It's that simple.

SECTION 13

The Default Dragon

Defaulting on a loan is when you stop making payments. After this, there is a short window to begin making payments again. When the window runs out, the collection calls start. This varies between loan types. I have witnessed collection calls and they are relentless. Do you really want to deal with someone calling constantly to hassle you about not paying your bills? Some of these collectors and organizations can help you consolidate and restructure your payment schedule, but I am not recommending that anyone default on student loan repayment. Before it gets to that point, explore all options and make decisions that are in the best interest of yourself and your family.

Defaulting on your student loans can land you in a deep, dark dungeon where I never want to see anyone default on student loans. It should not be considered a viable solution. The default dungeon will negatively impact your future credit score, purchasing power, wage garnishments, and future earning potential. Yes, the federal government and banks will garnish your wages, taxes, and even Social Security payments to collect on student loan debt owed. Do you really want to have garnishments from defaulted student loans at age 80? The answer is a resounding *no* for all us.

Before defaulting on loans, consider every available option and proactively work with the loan providers. The last thing the government or bank wants is for someone not to pay their bill. It's lost revenue. It will cost them money to send the debt to collections and pay someone to pester you for payment.

If you are struggling with payments, work with the loan provider. Ask for a supervisor or manager if a lower-level employee is not helpful or doesn't know the answers. Then work to design a plan that works for your situation. Have a direct conversation with the lender about the severity of your financial situation and how defaulting might be your only option. Most organizations will work with you if you are proactive and upfront regarding your financial situation.

It is not an easy conversation to have and many of us are embarrassed because we cannot make payments. There is no shame in asking for a plan as long as you are reinforcing the fact that you want to make payments but are currently unable to make the full, scheduled payment. The last thing that you or the organization wants is for you to default on a payment.

SECTION 14

Work to the Rescue?

Could student loan debt repayment programs be the new dental and vision insurance? In 2016, I was working as Interim Human Resources Director for a local hospital in upstate New York. One day, I thought about a program such as this for the hospital as a possible solution to address the high turnover rate in a few of the departments. I approached the talent acquisition manager about the idea, but they brushed it off. "We already have a program like that with a nursing school," they said. One nursing school? What about the 4,000+ other employees who work at the hospital? At the time, I really thought this was a great solution for reducing turnover and growing talent within this healthcare system.

On average, replacing an employee equals at least six months of salary lost. Companies invest in employees and have expectations of longevity and success. Relieving some of the stress caused by student loan debt is a perk that companies can offer to incentivize applicants to come to work for their organizations. Employers pioneering student loan repayment programs and other programs like these will be on the forefront of recruiting and retaining top talent, as the workforce continues to grow in competition.

The new employee perk is still in its infancy. More companies are now realizing the true potential of a program such as this and the importance of student loan debt management to the workforce. If an employee is stressed out due to compounding interest on student loan debt, how productive is that individual going to be in the workforce?

I believe there is tremendous value in offering such programs because this in the workforce addressing younger employees. Tuition reimbursement has been offered by companies for decades, but most jobs require at a minimum a four-year degree to be considered. What good is tuition reimbursement if they require a degree before you can even apply?

For those of us looking for alternative options, there are a few places that offer student loan repayment for relocation.

Below are relocation options:

- 50 counties in Kansas - save up to $15,000.00 in student loan debt
- Niagara Falls, New York - save up to $7,000.00 in student loan debt
- Saskatchewan, Canada - save up to $20,000.00 in student loan debt

I do foresee more areas in the future offering relocation packages to workers in hopes of bringing in a young and educated workforce. As more places see the value in a relocation program, more options will become available. Kansas might not be your first relocation option, but free money is free money.

Companies will specify employee benefits and perks on their websites. A benefit like this will stand out on one of those pages. What if your dream company doesn't offer a student loan repayment perk? Did you ask about alternative options? Perhaps a sign-on bonus, pay for performance, a bonus after

90 days of employment, or a different perk? What is the worst thing they can do? Tell you no! If you don't ask, you will never know.

Remember, if you do accept the repayment perk or a bonus, many organizations have repayment periods. You will have to repay money to them as well if you leave early. If the company provides $5000 to repay student loans and requires a twenty-four month commitment, be prepared to work there for twenty-four months. If you leave after six or twelve months, you will owe a prorated amount. As usual, read the fine print in the policy and ask questions upfront.

SECTION 15

Know Your Options

Companies and the government offering options of loan repayment assistance will continue to be a growing trend. It's time to get personal about student loan debt. Once I complete my third Master's degree, I will review all options regarding my debt and decide from there what will be the best course of action.

My student loan debts stand as this:

Syracuse MBA:

Borrowed 117,000

2018 Paid: $51,000 in student loans

2019 Paid: Estimate $37-$38,000

Tulane (3rd Master's) Anticipated Graduation 2021:

2019 Borrowed $12,000

2019 Paid $6,000

Friends have been denied consolidation due to credit rating issues. If you do not have an outstanding credit score, bank consolidation acceptance is unlikely. Making payments on time on everything is critical to an outstanding credit score. If you want to consolidate, know your credit score and review options.

Personal Loans

Securing a personal loan through a bank to cover a smaller amount of student loan debt may be an alternative option. That said, I do not imagine a bank lending $100,000 on a private loan to pay off student loans. The risk is too high because of bankruptcy. The financial institution might, however, consider $10,000 or $15,000 in a personal loan, which could greatly reduce your interest rate and help you build a relationship with a local bank. As always, if you don't do your research and ask, you will never know.

Second Mortgage

What about rolling your student loan debt into a mortgage? I do know of people who have done this as well. My only concern is how long do you want to take to pay off a degree? While this will reduce your interest rate and consolidate the debt into one payment, I would tread cautiously with the amount you add to the mortgage debt you agree to.

Credit Card Transfers

Credit card payments will not work. People were doing this and then filing bankruptcy on the credit cards. It sounds like a nice scam, but companies and the government caught up with it.

Debt Consolidation Companies

Student loan debt consolidation is a big business and companies are making tremendous profits off of other people's debt. Why pay someone a fee when you can apply on your own? The choice is yours, but that money could be better spent paying down debt. Avoid student loan debt consolidation companies and do the work for yourself. It saves you money and will provide you a better understanding of what is required. Maybe one day you will be able to help someone else through the process.

In the end, you, your spouse or your family must make decisions that will benefit your financial well-being. Don't lose sight of the people who are there to support your decisions and to guide you through the process.

Do your research and ask questions. The more options you have, the easier the decision will be in the end. Think creatively and write down ideas and solutions. It might sound crazy, but then again, it might work.

SECTION 16

How to Defeat the Dragon

Because us Millennials seek recognition and acknowledgment for our accomplishments, I want to congratulate you on your education and thank you for taking the time to read this book. This is not a simple problem we as Millennials face. The amount of student loan debt continues to grow both for our generation and Generation Z. We must prove people wrong and make fiscally responsible choices as we grow. We can defeat the student loan dragon.

We live in an "I want it now" world but we can't always have it right now. Learning to live within a budget and become disciplined on decisions is the only option we have. If you make $100,000 but spend $150,000 how far will you get in life?

Student loan debt is awful. There is no denying that. But it is important to remember that you agreed to the terms when you signed the paperwork. No one forced you to sign the loan document. You made a decision and invested in your education. Right or wrong, it is now your debt. I agree with everyone that college is completely overpriced, but I made my choice time after time and signed the loan paperwork.

I want to continue my education because I have seen the investment pay off in the end and know that the trend will continue. There is no chance of changing the past, but you can control the future by how you manage your debt. Live below your means and follow a disciplined budget. Network with others who have student loan debt and listen to everyone, but be critical of what advice you follow.

Will the government wipe out student loan debt and ensure college is free for everyone? Maybe. However, nothing is truly free, even if politicians tell you it is. Someone will end up paying for it. Politicians today have little experience with the stress and overwhelming pressure of managing the levels of debt our generation has incurred. Keep this in mind if you are waiting for complete loan forgiveness from the government. Why should we listen to or believe anything they say about student loan debt and restructuring programs? The government is making billions of dollars in revenue off student loan interest. It is now a great source of revenue for them. The solution for us is to minimize the interest that we owe on the debt and break the system. If they are not making money off the interest, the revenue stream will stop.

There is no magic wand or simple fix to overcoming the current student loan problem. I do not have an answer for the politicians or legislators who have allowed this problem to grow and grow. I do have suggestions on how we as a nation, approach our options in the future:

- Cap the amount of student loan debt an individual can borrow.
- Lower the interest rates! Working professionals who I know with law degrees and master's degrees who went to college in the 1990s are locked in at 1% and 2%. Why can't we as Millennials have the same interest rates? The government and banks would still make money, but they'd be giving us a better chance to reduce our debt.

- Revamp the financial aid system. It should include accountability metrics, suspension of benefits, and equality throughout the system based not only on need, but achievement. If you fail a course, the financial aid should be suspended for six or twelve months. Individuals applying for financial aid should be required to write essays and put in additional work to receive aid like with scholarship applications. Implement rules related to GPA and financial performance when borrowing money or receiving financial aid. If you fail four out of four courses, why should you be allowed to borrow? Borrowing privileges should be extended based on expectations and performance.
- Extend the six-month repayment free window to ten or twelve months to allow graduates the opportunity to establish themselves in a career or make career changes.

- Consider more repayment programs, relocation programs, volunteer programs, and disaster relief programs.
- Force colleges to charge less money!
- Hold everyone accountable, and provide information and resources more readily.

These simple suggestions would not be the solution to everyone's student loan debt problem. They would not solve all the problems we face in this country with student loan debt. However, something must be done. We are currently only seeing the tip of the iceberg for the effect of student loan debt over the next 20, 30, or 40 years. Does anyone really think Millennials will have purchasing power for new houses, cars, or sending their own children to college if they are still drowning in student loan debt at age 50 or 60?

Some of us received partial or full scholarships for college. As more students are now taking on increased levels of student loan debt, college endowments will suffer. That can hurt our kids and grandkids for future scholarships. Endowments are important to colleges and universities.

If you follow my advice, you won't have to live a lifetime of debt. Do things that others will not do. Sacrifice, live below your means, and make smart choices. The choice is yours. I want to see every one of you live a student loan debt-free life. Don't let the dragon slay you. Defeat the dragon!

Will the next presidential election make a difference?

Before starting this section Google "government revenue made off student loan interest". In 0.71 seconds, I received 21,000,000 links related to this topic. That's up from .43 seconds and 2,700,000 when I wrote the first edition of this book! Note that the figures will vary based on the media source and year. Still, the number is astounding. The amount of revenue that is made off student loan debt by the government is significant. Regardless of which political party you support or who you will or did vote for in any given election, the numbers do not lie. The government must disclose this information to the public.

In late 2016, President Obama signed a bill to eliminate $108 billion in student loan debt. The relief program has no effect on my debt, and I will not qualify for any elimination of current debt (at this time). Research the program and understand if there are options that you can take advantage of regarding the current rules and regulation changes. Remember one thing about this program, someone will pay for it. Yes, we do need to overhaul the system, but taxpayers are now picking up the bill for $108 billion in student loan debt. That means you and I are paying for this regardless.

On the Republican side, then President-Elect Trump proposed education reform as part of his campaign. Fast forward to March 18, 2019 and The Chronicle of Higher Education ran an article about The White House releasing its first stand-alone proposal for higher-education reform that urged the U.S. Congress to enact laws affecting accreditation, Pell Grants, and student-loan repayment (Johnson, S. (2019, March 18). Here's What the Trump Administration Wants to Change in Higher Ed's Landmark Law. (Retrieved from https://www.chronicle.com/article/Here-s-What-the-Trump/245919).

Trump's budget proposal for 2020, released earlier that month, included a $7 billion cut in the U.S. Department of

Education, a changed student-loan repayment process, and the elimination of the Public Service Loan Forgiveness program. The proposal also alludes to risk-sharing, the idea that colleges should share financial responsibility for student loans. An alternative to public-service loan forgiveness, Trump's proposal suggests, could be forgiving all undergraduate student loans after 180 months of income-driven repayment. Lastly, the White House also suggested limiting Direct PLUS loans, which the federal government offers to graduate students and parents, which congressional Republicans have targeted before.

There is No Crystal Ball

Will these reforms eventually occur? Time will tell. If you review the figures above, why would any politician want to make changes to a system that is generating billions of dollars in additional revenue?

Each political change might result in significant changes to the student loan process for future students. However, what about those who are struggling with their debt now? What happens to us? We continue to sacrifice and make fiscally responsible decisions to live a student loan debt-free life. I personally do not expect any president or politician to reduce my student loan debt. Would I welcome it? That depends. I know someone will pay for it through taxes, either this generation or the next generation. Do not expect significant changes to the system. Make the best choice for your life and your family. Defeating the student loan dragon is dependent on your choices. Make sure you are making fiscally responsible choices to set yourself up for a strong financial future.

SECTION 17

Finding Your Happily Ever After

The journey is not easy, but every journey begins with the first step. I have lived with student loan debt, conquered student loan debt, and now I am living with it once again. I am a glutton for punishment, or as my former professor says, "You don't learn your lesson, do you?" The process takes extreme discipline, self-control, and sacrifice. You alone can make the choice on whether or not having a college education is the right investment for your future. If you are willing to sacrifice and work constantly to pay down the debt, you can be financially successful.

I know without a doubt that we can all live debt-free lives through making smart decisions, utilizing discipline, and making sacrifices. This book is focused on student loan debt and questions to consider before signing on the dotted line. The habits, decisions, and sacrifices involved should be considered for all financial choices we face throughout life. Know the difference between a need and a want but keep in mind this will vary depending on the person and the situation. I cannot answer that question for you, but make sure that you are supporting your financial goals and that you are not just creating a $200 bar tab you must charge.

Whether you are applying to your first college or finishing your second master's degree, the choices you make in life are yours to make. Just because the loan repayment terms say thirty years does not mean you need to pay the loan off for thirty years. Do the math. Calculate out the interest and see how much you will pay after thirty years versus a shorter period. Remember, what will your degree be worth in thirty years?

By reading this book you have already taken an excellent step towards a debt-free life. Now you must decide on how you take the second step. After you are successful in paying off your student loan debt, you might be offering advice to me or someone else who is in debt! I want to hear your stories of success.

You are well on your way to financial freedom. Living without debt is living a less stressful life. If you take one thing away from this book let it be this: You must be willing to do things that others will not do. Pay off your debt, and do what others cannot.

Good luck and enjoy your journey! Once you destroy your debt, I want to hear about it. Please send me your stories at Matthew@burrconsultingllc.com and share your thoughts on a life free of student loan debt.

SECTION 18

A Strategy That Slays

I will leave you with my final summary list of advice to get you started on developing a plan that works:

- ❏ Research, research, research. Know the costs involved of the college you want to attend, understand the student loans, and payment requirements. Ask questions and be prepared with information.

- ❏ Set up a budget by starting with making a list using a spreadsheet or system that works for you including all the debt you have (student, credit card, vehicle, mortgage, medical, etc.). Develop a schedule for all your debt and monthly expenses. Track every purchase you make. There are some great apps that can help with this.

❏ Draft a plan to repay the highest interest debt first (month by month) and commit to making two payments a month if you can.

❏ Discipline yourself to focus on the budget and repayment plan for six months. If it isn't working, look at why, break it down, and rebuild it.

❏ If you have more than two credit cards, cut them up. Why have extra debt at your fingertips? Credit cards are fake money and the companies love when people charge, charge, charge. I use cards for purchases almost daily, but make payments every week. That means I win and take complete advantage of the miles and cash back without ever paying a dime more than I need.

- ❏ Consolidate credit card debt and other debt, if possible. Explore all of your options with balance transfers.

- ❏ Know what future employers could be offering in terms of benefits and perks. The more you know, the easier it will be to make a responsible choice. Ask questions because your future employer may offer perks you don't know about.

- ❏ Talk about your plan and write it down. The more people you tell about your goal of living a debt-free life, the more likely you will be to stay focused on the goal.

- ❏ Talk to older people. Both of my grandmothers lived through the Great Depression, and they have given me the best financial advice on savings, budgeting, and making smart choices. If you think we have it difficult now, talk to someone who lived through the Great Depression. That should scare you enough to focus.

- ❏ Ask for help. If you are unclear on how to develop a budget or want someone else to review your debt, just ask. Ask a family member, friend, financial advisor, or someone at the local bank to help you. Obviously, the goal is to get this done for free, but what is the time value of money? Take the individual to lunch or dinner to thank them for the help. Setup six-month reviews with them to help you stay disciplined.
- ❏ Think creatively. Explore every option possible and then make a decision that works for you and your family.
- ❏ Do not view failure as failure. If you make a mistake, learn from the mistake and move on. The only true failure is not learning from a mistake.

❏ Reward yourself for small accomplishments and small victories. No, I do not mean take a trip to Hawaii and spend $6,000 or $7,000 on a luxury vacation. Go out for a special dinner or spend the weekend somewhere nice, but think cheap.

This is your life; shape it before someone else does. You control your future. Make the choices to put you able to live the life you want. Dream of a future life and then go work for it! Work very hard for it. We all have that ability, all it takes is discipline, determination, willpower, hard work, and sacrifice. I have no doubt you can and will live a debt-free life.

Stay on top of your debt. As you watch it dwindle, like I do every day, you'll find it to be a rewarding experience. Yes, it can be overwhelming, especially when the car needs new brakes, but watching those numbers go down now so your savings account numbers can go up later is well worth it!

AUTHOR BIOGRAPHY

Mathew W. Burr, MBA, MHRIR, GPHR, SHRM-SCP, SPHR, CPHR

ABOUT:
Matthew Burr has over 13-years of experience working in the human resources field, starting his career as an Industrial Relations Intern at Kennedy Valve Manufacturing to most recently founding and managing a human resource consulting company; Burr Consulting, LLC and Co-Owner of Labor Love, a Labor and Employment Law poster printing company. Prior to founding the consulting firm, the majority of his career was spent in manufacturing and healthcare. He specializes in labor and employment law, conflict resolution, performance management, labor and employment relations. Matthew has a generalist background in HR and provides strategic HR services to his clients, focusing on small and medium sized organizations. In July 2017, Matthew started as an Associate Professor of Business Administration at Elmira College and was promoted into the Continuing Education & Business Administration Department Liaison role in July 2018. He teaches both undergraduate and graduate level business courses at Elmira College. Matthew is also the SHRM Certification Exam Instructor at the college, his students currently have an 80% pass rate on the SHRM-SCP and 92.3% pass rate on the SHRM-CP. Matthew works as a trainer Tompkins Cortland Community College, Corning Community College, Broome Community College and Penn State University. He also acts as an On-Call Mediator and Fact-Finder through the Public Employment Relations Board in New York State, working with public sector employers and labor unions.

PUBLICATIONS:
Matthew has publications at the Cornell HR Review, Business Insider, New York State Bar Association (NYSBA), Society of

Human Resource Management (SHRM), Expert 360 (in Australia). In early 2017, he published his first book, "$74,000 in 24 Months: How I killed my student loans (and you can too!)."

VOLUNTEER WORK:
Matthew is currently the New York State Society of Human Resource Management (NYSSHRM) District Director of the Southern District, President of the Human Resource Association of the Twin Tiers (HRATT), a board member for the Community Dispute Resolution Center (CDRC) and Boy Scouts of America (BSA) Merit Badge Counselor.

EDUCATION & TRAINING:
Matthew has an associate degree in business administration from Tompkins Cortland Community College, a Bachelor of Science degree in business management from Elmira College, a master's degree from the University of Illinois School of Labor and Employment Relations in Human Resources & Industrial Relations and a Master's in Business Administration specializing in entrepreneurship from Syracuse University. He currently holds a Lean Six Sigma Green Belt, Senior Professional in Human Resources (SPHR), Global Professional in Human Resources (GPHR), Society of Human Resource Management Senior Certified Professional (SHRM-SCP) and the Chartered Professional in Human Resources (CPHR) certifications. Matthew is currently pursuing a Master of Jurisprudence in Labor & Employment Law through the Tulane University Law School, anticipated graduation May 2021.

FEATURED IN & ON:
Matthew has been featured on CNN Money, Fast Company, Fits Small Business, Magnify Money, Monster.com, My Twin Tiers, Namely, Student Loan Hero, Smart Sheet and CEO Blog Nation, Human Resource Certification Institute (HRCI), Society of Human Resource Management (SHRM).

Made in the USA
Coppell, TX
21 January 2021